In the Middle *of* the Mess

In the Middle *of* the Mess

STRENGTH FOR THIS BEAUTIFUL, BROKEN LIFE

STUDY GUIDE

SIX SESSIONS

Sheila Walsh

With Ashley Wiersma

ZONDERVAN®

In the Middle of the Mess Study Guide

Published in Nashville, Tennessee, by Nelson Books, an imprint of Thomas Nelson. Nelson Books and Thomas Nelson are registered trademarks of HarperCollins Christian Publishing, Inc.

Author is represented by the literary agency of Alive Communications, Inc., 7680 Goddard Street, Suite 200, Colorado Springs, CO 80920, www.alivecommunications.com.

Thomas Nelson titles may be purchased in bulk for educational, business, fundraising, or sales promotional use. For information, please e-mail SpecialMarkets@ThomasNelson.com.

ISBN 978-0-310-08943-8

First Printing September 2017 / Printed in the United States of America

Contents

How to Use This Guide

Group Size

The *In the Middle of the Mess* video study is designed to be experienced in a group setting such as a Bible study, Sunday school class, or other small-group gathering. If the gathering is large, your leader may wish to split everyone into smaller groups of five or six people to make sure everyone has enough time to participate in discussions.

Materials Needed

Everyone in your group will need his or her own copy of this study guide, which includes the opening question(s) you will discuss, notes for the video segments, group discussion questions, prompts for closing prayer, and personal studies that you and the group members will complete between sessions. You will also want a copy of the *In the Middle of the Mess* book, which provides further insights into the material you are covering in this study. (See the note at the end of each week's personal study for specific chapters to read in the book to prepare for the next week's group meeting.)

Facilitation

Your group will need to appoint a person to serve as a facilitator. This person will be responsible for starting the video and keeping track of time during discussions and activities. Facilitators may also ready questions aloud and monitor discussions, prompting participants to respond and ensuring that everyone has the opportunity to participate. If you have been chosen for this role, there are additional instructions and resources in the back of this guide to help you lead your group members through the study.

Personal Studies

During the week, you can maximize the impact of the study with the personal studies provided for each session. Each of these personal studies is broken into three parts that will help you to revisit your experience with the group that week, receive God's truth through studying the Bible, and reorient your habits and heart to bring the theme of each day's study to life. The final section in each personal study will help you practice the discipline that Sheila is discussing that week as she leads you and your group members through the journey of brokenness. Treat each personal study like a devotional and use them in whatever way works best for you. You could do one section each day for three days of the week or complete them all in one sitting.

Session One

Brokenness Is the Beginning

Grace and Radical Acceptance

You will know the truth, and the truth will set you free.

John 8:32 ESV

Session Overview

It's there to greet you first thing in the morning, through an unkind word from your spouse or child. It's there again as you merge onto the highway, via the other guy's blaring horn, causing your unwanted swerve. It shows up in your friend's phone call . . . there's an edge there—you can hear it. Things aren't as they should be. News stories shouted at you all day long only confirm what you suspected to be true: *things are not okay in this world.* Life is broken—deeply broken—shattered into a million pieces. The question isn't so much, "Is there brokenness in this world?" for that response would be *yes*. The question is, "What will we do with this brokenness in the world . . . and also, in *me*?"

In this opening session, we'll journey through the Word of God to take a look at both the expected and unexpected nature of this brokenness that so marks our existence. What did God promise would be true of our earthly lives? How did those whose lives are detailed in Scripture move through seasons of trial with wisdom and grace? And, if we believe God truly can bring beauty from ashes, as the prophet Isaiah so boldly declared (see Isaiah 61:3), then how are we to find our way from here to there, from the bleakness and desperation that marks brokenness's beginning to the longed-for victory that we are promised?

Come. Sit with God. Soak in His Word. Let His ages-old perspective and promises sink deep into your sea-tossed soul. There is a marvelous end game to this brokenness that we're just *sure* will do us in. Brokenness is a necessary beginning. This is where our discussion begins.

Opening Thoughts

Take one to two minutes to open your time together with prayer. Then, have each group member answer the following question before watching the video segment:

How have you seen "brokenness" show up in your life? Describe for your group a recent encounter or exchange from which you walked away thinking, *Things here aren't as they are meant to be.*

Video: Brokenness Is the Beginning (20 MINUTES)

Play the video for Session 1. Use the following prompts to record your thoughts as you watch.

VIDEO NOTES

Secrets don't keep us safe

God's rock-solid promise

Six truths

Where true transformation comes from

The great distance between our head and our heart

Imprisoned to be set free

Two benefits to coming to the end of oneself

The usefulness of “radical acceptance”

Everyone who calls on God is saved by God

The one-word prayer “Jesus”

Letter from a devoted daughter

Group Discussion

Spend the balance of your group time answering as many of the following questions as you have time and energy for, being sure to give equal opportunity for each member to share.

1. Briefly review your video notes. Given your present circumstances, what word, phrase, sentiment, or concept feels most relevant to you? Why?

2. Sheila noted the six sessions of this study. Which of the following holds the most promise for you? Which one makes you feel anxious the first time you read it?

    - *Brokenness is the beginning* . . . the truth of our situation, as bleak as that truth may be, can set us free.
    - *Brokenness is hard* . . . even on the darkest night, we never walk the path of grief alone.
    - *Brokenness is loud* . . . even in our noisy world, we can learn to live in the stillness and quietness of God's presence.
    - *Brokenness is to be shared* . . . there is strength to be found in confessing our sins to one another.
    - *Brokenness is the path to healing* . . . when we fix our eyes on God, we live a life of thanksgiving.
    - *Brokenness is temporary* . . . what you are facing right now will pass.

3. In what way can you relate to Sheila's experience of raw emotions resurfacing long after you thought those feelings were dealt with and buried? Why is jagged-edge brokenness so terribly hard to "get over"? Do you believe it's possible to *truly move past* deep pain?

4. What thoughts came to mind when you heard Sheila reference this session's spiritual-discipline focus of *radical acceptance*? What does that practice involve? What would you gain from the practice of radically accepting your present circumstances and pain?

5. Sheila said one of her biggest motivations for putting together the content for this study was to remind people that "even in our brokenness, we can tell the truth . . . we don't have to hide anymore." What do you suppose keeps us from telling our truth? What keeps us hiding from the reality of our lives?

6. What attitudes, actions, or habits might the group practice in order to encourage your honest participation in this six-session experience? What do they need to understand about you in this process?

Closing Prayer

Taking as much time as your group needs, have each member who feels comfortable complete the following prayer prompt as a way to close your discussion:

God, please let this present brokenness I'm dealing with be the beginning of . . .

Between-Sessions Personal Study

Session One

Reflect on the content you've discussed this week by engaging in any or all of the following between-sessions personal studies. The time you invest will be well spent, so let God use it to draw you closer to Him. At your next meeting, share with your group any key points or insights that stood out to you as you spent this time with the Lord.

PART ONE:
The Existence of Brokenness Is Expected

Where does it come from, that immediate regret you feel when you respond too harshly to a loved one or that sorrow over someone being harsh with *you*? Why is it there, that sense of insecurity when it seems everyone else has their lives together, that frustration that things haven't panned out like you thought they would? What do you call that anxiety over not having enough money to cover your obligations, or that fear that your kids aren't turning out right, or the resignation to the fact that three glasses of wine has become part of your nightly routine? The answer to these and a thousand more questions is found in a single word: *brokenness*. Brokenness is a declaration that all is not as it should be in the world, the realization that we indeed have fallen . . . and are having trouble getting back up.

REVISIT YOUR EXPERIENCE

Take a few moments to revisit this week's teaching as it relates to your personal experience.

When you think of the word *brokenness,* what thoughts or images come to mind? What experiences or assumptions influence these associations for you?

As you survey the landscape of your life today, where do you spot brokenness in any of its forms?

What emotions bubble up to the surface of your mind and heart as you focus your attention on these aspects of brokenness you face?

If you were to focus on *one particular aspect of brokenness* for the purposes of this study, what would it be? Select one from the options that follow on the next page, or write in a one-to two-word phrase that describes the brokenness you feel. (You can go back and apply the practices introduced in this guide to additional aspects of brokenness you'd like repaired, but to aid your focus this first time through, consider choosing just one.)

- ☐ Abuse
- ☐ Addiction
- ☐ Anxiety/anxious thoughts
- ☐ Chronic pain
- ☐ Debilitating fear
- ☐ Depression
- ☐ Distance from loved ones
- ☐ Escapist thoughts
- ☐ Family member's pain
- ☐ Financial debt
- ☐ God seems silent
- ☐ Grief over loss
- ☐ Grief over world affairs
- ☐ Illness
- ☐ Impact-hungry
- ☐ Job dissatisfaction
- ☐ Job loss
- ☐ Lack of material resources
- ☐ Loneliness
- ☐ Marital strife/discord
- ☐ Overwhelmed with life
- ☐ Pain from physical accident
- ☐ Parenting challenges
- ☐ Post-traumatic stress
- ☐ Prodigal child
- ☐ Sorrow
- ☐ Spiritual doubts
- ☐ Substance misuse
- ☐ Suffering
- ☐ Suicidal thoughts
- ☐ Tragedy
- ☐ Trauma
- ☐ Uncertainty regarding future
- ☐ Unwanted health diagnosis
- ☐ Other ____________________

With this singular aspect of brokenness in mind, use the following prompts to describe the effect it is having on the various parts of your life:

Relational

Emotional

Physical

Psychological

Vocational

Financial

Marital

Spiritual

Other

Does anything shock you about the level of impact your brokenness is having on you? Which aspects have you just "come to expect" as being part of your life here on earth? Note your thoughts in the space below.

This is one of the sad conditions of life, that experience is not transmissible. No man will learn from the suffering of another; he must suffer himself.

—JAMES H. AUGHEY

RECEIVE GOD'S TRUTH

Read each of the following Scripture passages and reflect on the related questions.

> Therefore, just as sin entered the world through one man, and death through sin, and in this way death came to all people, because all sinned—to be sure, sin was in the world before the law was given, but sin is not charged against anyone's account where there is no law.
>
> (Romans 5:12–13)

Who do you understand the "one man" to be (see also Genesis 3)? How did sin first enter our world?

What accompanied sin as it came into the picture here on earth?

Who is affected by the "death" that has arrived?

Given that you and everyone around you are alive today, what type of "death" is ushered in through sin?

How does spiritual death lead to a sense that "things are broken" here on earth?

> We all, like sheep, have gone astray, each of us has turned to our own way; and the LORD has laid on him the iniquity of us all.
>
> (ISAIAH 53:6)

Who is tempted to go his or her own way, according to this verse?

Why is going one's own way considered going "astray"?

What is the connection between humankind's tendency to go its own way and the fact that brokenness exists in the world?

> "He will wipe every tear from their eyes. There will be no more death" or mourning or crying or pain, for the old order of things has passed away.
>
> (Revelation 21:4)

What can you deduce about our present reality, given this picture of glory that John paints in Revelation?

What type of "death" is John speaking of here?

What confidence do you gain from John's vision of the future for those who are in Christ?

It's okay not to be okay.

—SHEILA WALSH

REORIENT YOUR HABITS AND HEART

As a means for bringing the first theme to life—that of brokenness being an expected part of our experience here on earth—select one or more of the following to practice sometime today:

- Sit with the concept from Isaiah 53:6 about the link between going your own way and the existence of brokenness. What brokenness have you known in your past that could have been averted had you submitted your will and ways to God?
- Write out the word *brokenness* on a sheet of paper. Create an acrostic based on your present challenges, forming a new word with each letter, such as "bleak days" for *b*, "repetition of previous mistakes" for *r*, and so forth. Read your acrostic aloud to yourself as a means of acknowledging the pain you've endured.
- Consider how brokenness sounds. What type of music, sound from nature, tone of voice, or other sound characterizes pain, in your view? Spend a few moments silently "playing" that sound in your mind. What emotions does the sound elicit from you?
- What are a few things you expect to transpire in a given week? A regular meeting at work, perhaps, or a child's school routine? The Tuesday-night neighborhood potluck, weekend worship at church, or book club on Thursday night? Jot down these events that occur each and every week. Now imagine what it would be like to actually slot "face challenges, obstacles, and pain" on your calendar. What would it be like to accept as usual, normal, and expected the brokenness that Scripture says we will undoubtedly endure?
- Go outside and find a few blades of grass, a small pile of leaves, or a stray feather. Toss one of these natural elements into the air and watch it float away in the wind. Thank God that someday, according to Revelation 21, every bit of brokenness we experience will fade, as though carried off by the wind. Imagine the future scene that John painted: no more death, no more crying, no more pain. What do you most look forward to about living in that new reality?

PART TWO:
The Experience of Brokenness Is Unexpected

Even if we embrace the idea that *general* brokenness is to be considered an expected part of life—something that is just part of existing in a fallen world—the *particular brokenness* we face still always seems to catch us off-guard. As Sheila mentioned during this week's teaching, the death of her mother brought to the surface all of the brokenness and pain she experienced when her dad died more than five decades before.

REVISIT YOUR EXPERIENCE

In general terms, how have you responded to the various troubling situations you've faced? On the grid below, note a handful of the biggest trials you've endured and your reaction to each.

Trial I Faced	How I Responded

Take another look at the grid above. Which of the situations you noted was most surprising to you? Why?

In what ways did this particular challenge go against how you thought your life would turn out?

Why is it easier to accept the general *idea* of brokenness than to accept the specific ways in which it shows up in our lives?

RECEIVE GOD'S TRUTH

Read each of the following Scripture passages and reflect on the related questions.

> Dear friends, do not be surprised at the fiery ordeal that has come on you to test you, as though something strange were happening to you.
>
> (1 Peter 4:12)

Why is Peter's "encouragement" so difficult to follow about receiving trials without feeling surprised?

Peter acknowledges that our tendency when trials come our way is to act as though "something strange" were happening to us. Based on the information you wrote on page 24, do you tend to receive struggles as what's normal or as something strange?

If a close friend asked for your advice on how to stop pushing against a current trial as though it were "something strange," what would you say?

What assumptions or attitudes most often get in your *own* way when it comes to living out the advice you would offer your friend?

> So to keep me from becoming conceited because of the surpassing greatness of the revelations, a thorn was given me in the flesh, a messenger of Satan to harass me, to keep me from becoming conceited. Three times I pleaded with the Lord about this, that it should leave me.
>
> (2 Corinthians 12:7–8 ESV)

What types of challenges do you think this "thorn" of Paul's might have represented?

Why did God ask Paul to face such an arduous challenge?

Do you think that any of the challenges you've faced have been "given to you by God" for a specific purpose? Why or why not?

What does the fact Paul begged God to take away the thorn reveal about Paul's level of expectation regarding that thorn?

How does your own resistance to the struggles you encounter reveal your expectations of life? If you had to name these expectations, what words would you use? Expectations of comfort, perhaps? Or of good health? Of financial resourcefulness? Of life-giving relationships? Of grateful children? Of peace?

REORIENT YOUR HABITS AND HEART

To help activate the theme of receiving instead of resisting struggles that come your way, select one or more of the following to practice sometime today:

- Carve out two or three minutes when you can sit still in a quiet spot, alone. With your life's most significant struggle in mind, shift your posture so that your arms are outstretched and your hands are upturned to heaven. Imagine yourself physically "receiving" the struggle into your hands, sensing the weight of it, the gravity of it, the force. Consider how it feels to draw it near instead of pushing it away—what emotions rise to the surface for you? What images does the burden bring forth? Sit with this present reality for a few moments. Ask Christ to be with you in the middle of the mess before leaving your seat and reentering your day.
- Spend some time journaling about your present pain. What expectations of your life does this challenge violate? What aspects of it feel totally unjust? In what ways does it feel like a "thorn" in your flesh?
- Read the full text of 1 Peter 4, noting the evidences of brokenness you find there as well as the stated purpose for the existence of pain. What encouragement can you take from Peter's words regarding the universal nature of pain?

PART THREE:
We Can Look to Jesus in Our Brokenness

For the Christ follower, the answer to all difficult and heartbreaking questions lies in the person of Jesus—His flawless nature, His boundless wisdom, and the faithful example He set. So, in each session, you will find an invitation to look to and learn from Him.

Recall that it wasn't until Sheila had exhausted every other option she could find and turned intentionally toward Jesus—"not just parts of me," she wrote, but "all of me, fully and faithfully"—that she could begin to find relief from the incredible pain she bore. This is the "beginning" we spoke of at the start of this session, the beginning that brokenness imparts. It's the beginning of a journey toward deeper intimacy with Jesus, an intimacy that we can know no other way.

What Jesus will show in this segment is that in order to knit ourselves to the heart of the Father, we must accept the pain the Father allows. "Radical acceptance," as behavioral therapists have called it, is the act of acknowledging not what we *wish* to be but rather what *actually is*.

REVISIT YOUR EXPERIENCE

What do you imagine "radical acceptance" would involve as it relates to your present round of suffering or challenges? Check the following response that best fits your definition:

- ☐ Letting the one who offended me off the hook
- ☐ Raising the white flag of surrender
- ☐ Pretending that nothing is wrong and moving on
- ☐ Changing my self-talk to something a little more positive
- ☐ Acknowledging the pain that I feel is present, it is real, and it really hurts

As it turns out, practicing "radical acceptance" has nothing to do with sticking your head in the sand, acting like nothing is the matter, giving up altogether, or simply altering what you say to yourself. Radical acceptance, as Sheila clarified in the video, is simply *seeing your suffering and calling it what it is*, so you consider how you'd like it to change.

Radical acceptance doesn't mean that we approve of our brokenness. It simply means that we see it. We quit stuffing it all the way down.

—SHEILA WALSH

What alternatives to radical acceptance have you practiced along the way—attempts to *not see* and *not name* the pain you feel? Denial, perhaps? Numbing yourself with substances or distractions? Blaming the one who hurt you? Refusing to put words to your pain? Note your thoughts in the space below before moving on.

How helpful have those alternatives been to you in allowing you to heal from the pain you feel? Explain.

What fears, insecurities, or lack of knowledge have kept you from pursuing radical acceptance of your particular brokenness as a path toward wholeness, holiness, and grace?

What do you fear being asked to relinquish should you choose to follow this "radical acceptance" course of action? Control? Pride? Independence from God? Something else?

RECEIVE GOD'S TRUTH

The most powerful example of a person radically accepting suffering and pain occurred in the moments before the crucifixion of Jesus Christ. You likely know this turn of events by heart. The Feast of the Unleavened Bread (the Passover) was nearing, and those in power plotted to take Jesus's life. One of Jesus's closest followers, Judas Iscariot, agreed to tell the leaders where Jesus was located in exchange for a few coins (a betrayal that had to cut deep). Jesus instituted the Lord's Supper, demonstrating the physical, bodily brokenness that was about to occur. And then we come to this scene, as recorded by Luke. Read the passage below and answer the questions that follow.

> Jesus went out as usual to the Mount of Olives, and his disciples followed him. On reaching the place, he said to them, "Pray that you will not fall into temptation." He withdrew about a stone's throw beyond them, knelt down and prayed, "Father, if you are willing, take this cup from me; yet not my will, but yours be done." An angel from heaven appeared to him and strengthened him. And being in anguish, he prayed more earnestly, and his sweat was like drops of blood falling to the ground.
>
> When he rose from prayer and went back to the disciples, he found them asleep, exhausted from sorrow. "Why are you sleeping?" he asked them. "Get up and pray so that you will not fall into temptation."
>
> (Luke 22:39–46)

Imagine that you were Jesus at the end of that very long day. How would you most likely have responded, given the heavy burden you were made to bear?

What emotions do you expect Jesus was experiencing as He prayed, "Father, if you are willing, take this cup from me; yet not my will, but yours be done"?

How does such a prayer reflect the idea of "radical acceptance"?

What type of strength do you suppose the angel who appeared afforded Jesus just after He had uttered those words? Why would that type of strength have been necessary to Him?

How do you think Jesus felt upon realizing that His prayer team had all fallen asleep, even as He battled spiritual forces and sweat drops of blood?

How was Jesus able to rise and continue along the fearsome journey that awaited Him, given the gut-wrenching experience He'd just had?

Do you believe similar strength and power awaits anyone who accepts the cup of suffering as Jesus did? Why or why not?

REORIENT YOUR HABITS AND HEART

When Sheila arrived at the end of herself and her schemes for "getting through" her pain, she finally turned toward Jesus, words of radical acceptance on her lips. In her book *In the Middle of the Mess*, she writes:

> Christian had fallen fast asleep. Barry could tell I wasn't doing well and suggested I take a bath and relax. I couldn't. I told him I was fine and just needed a little alone time. As the night wore on, the house grew cold and still, and it felt as if evil had crawled through cracks in the wall. The evil seeped across the floorboards and down to my toes. It crept up my shins, up my torso, up my neck. It stuck to me.
>
> The weapon that night was a large knife. I saw it lying on the draining board in the kitchen, and the voices were deafening.
>
> *Just pick it up. It won't hurt. It will be over soon. You don't have to live like this anymore.*
>
> I walked into the living room and lay face down on the carpet. All I could say over and over was one name: "Jesus! Jesus! Jesus!"
>
> The hours passed—one o'clock, two o'clock. At three in the morning something inside me shifted. I remembered whose I was. I stood up and shouted out, "No!" I picked up a verse I've known since I was a child and wielded it like a weapon, "For everyone who calls on the name of the Lord will be saved" (Romans 10:13 HCSB).
>
> I called that verse aloud and believed it. I called on His name and believed Him. I had been saved from hell and into eternity as an eleven-year-old girl, when I accepted Jesus as my Savior. But that night, I needed saving in the present, and I knew it. It wasn't that I needed to become a Christian again; instead, I needed the power of the living Word of God to save me from the present tormentors.

> And that night, as I called on the name of the Lord, I found Him pushing back the darkness, the evil—all of those suicidal thoughts.
>
> I felt Him saving me.
>
> This is the truth I would discover that night: Christ came to save us in this present moment. The gift of salvation is God's active, present gift to us, no matter where we are.

This was the truth of Sheila's situation, a truth she hadn't been able to tell back when she hosted a show aimed at inviting *others* to tell their own. This was the suffering she'd struggled to accept, rising to the top of her consciousness and spilling right out. This was *radical acceptance* in its purest, rawest state, refusing to stuff the pain down further and instead letting it just. come. out. "You will know the truth," this session's epigraph boldly states, quoting the apostle John, "and the truth will set you free" (John 8:32).

I discovered in my darkest moments that sometimes the most powerful prayer of all is just a single word: "Jesus!"

—SHEILA WALSH

In what ways can you relate to Sheila's experience of coming to the end of herself and all of her efforts? Have you known yet what that feels like?

Who or what do you think protected Sheila from self-harm and outright destruction during those hours that passed by so slowly, before she finally called on the Lord?

What do you imagine happened both in heaven and on earth as soon as Sheila uttered that one-word prayer: "Jesus! Jesus! Jesus!"

What similarities and differences do you note between the account of Jesus Christ praying on the Mount of Olives and Sheila praying from the floor of her living room? Write down a few thoughts below.

Similarities	*Differences*

How would you have responded to that level of despair, had you faced Sheila's situation that night?

What emotions crop up in you as you consider engaging in the same process of radical acceptance that Sheila's story demonstrates?

In this session's video, Sheila confirmed that radical acceptance is not a one-time affair but a spiritual discipline to be practiced with the same fervency and frequency as other spiritual disciplines, such as contemplation, solitude, or prayer. As with any spiritual discipline, the *power is in the practice*, not in hyper-focusing on particular outcomes. We "pray without ceasing," for example, not so much because we feel like prayer all day, every day, at life's every twist and turn, but because we are practicing a life of constant communication with our heavenly Father. We are in training for righteousness's sake. Similarly, we must keep coming back to this practice of radical acceptance if we ever hope to heal. We must keep saying over and over, "I see you, suffering, I do. I *knew* you were there somewhere."

What follows in the final portion of this study is a series of "steps," if you will, to aid you in your practice of radical acceptance. But as with any spiritual practice, you should feel free to go wherever the Spirit leads. Don't get hung up on ticking off to-do boxes or turning the bullet points you find here into a stale and ritualized routine. Instead, simply use what follows as a guide, and then ask God to graciously lead.

PRACTICING THE DISCIPLINE OF RADICAL ACCEPTANCE

It is quite difficult in our results-oriented culture to sit with something difficult instead of skipping right to solution-seeking (even if that solution happens to be proclaiming, "Suffering? Me? No. Trust me—really—I'm *fine*."). But to know the usefulness of suffering—the character it forms in us, the glory it delivers to God, the empathy it affords us for others, and so forth—we must *first acknowledge that it exists*. And so: radical acceptance. It is with this practice that we say:

"I see you, suffering."

"I feel you, pain."

"Yes, this is actually happening to me."

"I didn't want this, but it is here."

And yet those words aren't said only to the air around us; no, they also are said to God. In the next session, we will explore the magnificent healing that begins to unfold, the moment we entrust our pain to God. But before that can happen, a certain transfer must occur, an exchange that begins by calling on one specific name.

"Father!" Jesus cried out.

"Jesus!" Sheila said that night.

Yes, transformation begins by calling on the Name above all other names.

1. Call on the Name of Jesus

Are you fed up with your own solutions and ready for real healing to occur? Simply call on the name of Jesus. Even if that is the extent of your prayer, say the name. Call His name. Beckon Him now.

"Jesus . . . Jesus . . . Jesus . . ."

Upon calling on the name of His Father, Jesus then reminded God of His pain. "I'm still carrying around this cup of suffering," He essentially said. "It's heavy. It's weighty. It's hard."

Without even knowing she was doing so, Sheila echoed this approach in that moment with Christ as she acknowledged the darkness, evil, and suicidal thoughts that had been plaguing her. Here, we find a level of honesty that can be agonizing to let play out.

2. Acknowledge the Pain

Are you tired of hiding and pretending, weary of acting as though nothing is wrong? It's time to exhale all falsehood and there, before God, *acknowledge the presence of pain.*

"I'm hurting . . ."
"I've failed again . . ."
"I can't arrest this addiction, Lord . . ."
"I'm desperate . . ."
"Life is hopeless . . ."
"I'll take any escape from this pain . . ."

Finally, after pouring out His pain and accepting the burden He was called to bear, Jesus made an incredible choice. He chose to stop fixating on the presence of pain and focus on His Father and the divine purpose for His life—a mission only He could fulfill. *This* was the power that carried Him from the garden to the agony of the cross.

For Sheila, this shift in focus felt like salvation—salvation that is available not only when we walk a church aisle or pray a beautiful prayer, but also in our quiet suffering, when our need for real rescue has shown itself once again.

The extreme greatness of Christianity lies in the fact that it does not seek a supernatural remedy for suffering, but a supernatural use for it.

—SIMONE WEIL

3. Turn to the Father

Are you in need of real rescue today? Turn your attention from the presence of the pain you've been carrying to the presence of your Father instead. He is near and He is listening. He holds all healing in His hands.

As you conclude your time in this session, spend a few moments logging your thoughts regarding "radically accepting" this suffering of yours. What parts of your present reality is it time for you to accept? What in your life needs "saving" and in what ways will Jesus accomplish that task? What subtle shifts in attitude or posture do you detect, as you practice focusing less on the presence of pain and more on the presence of God? What "strength" does God long to impart to you now, as you take this vital first step?

On the lined page that follows, consider adopting the response that Sheila herself did, which was to write a letter to her dad. Only, in this case, craft it to your *heavenly* Father. Tell Him all that is on your heart.

Before the next meeting, read chapters 3 and 4 of *In the Middle of the Mess.*

Session Two

Brokenness Is Hard

Honest Prayer and Grief

For my yoke is easy, and my burden is light.

MATTHEW 11:30 ESV

Session Overview

Even if you can accept the fact that in this world you will have trouble, you still have to wonder why that trouble has to weigh so much. The suffering, the pain, the disillusionment, the loss—how can you be expected to bear such a load?

This brokenness we've discovered, here in this fallen world, is heavy, and burdensome, and real. So it's no wonder that as you and I survey this mass, we long for deliverance from our mess. "How can I get this weight off of me?" we cry out, desperate for an ounce of relief. We look to people and substances and fantasies and TV—there's the escape hatch that we need! But in the end, we're still left heavy-laden. Is there any real relief to be found?

In this session, we will work through the difficult parts of our brokenness—why it's there, how it feels, and what we're to do to lighten the load. Is there a point to the burdens we've been bearing all this time? And, if so, might we ask what it is? As you go through this session, open your mind and your heart to the counsel of your loving Father, who longs for you to live burden-free.

Opening Thoughts

Take one to two minutes to open your time together with prayer. Then, have each group member answer the following questions before watching the video segment:

What is a highlight from your between-sessions learning that you would like to share with the group?

What is the heaviest thing you've tried to carry—physically, emotionally, or otherwise? How did your efforts work for you? What became of your bearing that load?

Video: Brokenness Is Hard (20.5 MINUTES)

Play the video for Session 2. Use the following prompts to record your thoughts as you watch.

VIDEO NOTES

Joyless in the midst of reasons for joy

When we need time and space to grieve

The hope offered to those who grieve in Christ

Our walls just keep us alone

Never separated from the love of God

The woman caught in adultery

No condemnation for those who are in Christ

Salvation as ongoing work

A father, a son, an altar

God's faithfulness to walk with you

The struggles and losses that we have known

Group Discussion

Spend the balance of your group time answering as many of the following questions as you have time and energy for, being sure to give equal opportunity for each member to share.

1. What is one theme, phrase, or idea you hope you remember from this session's video content? Why was it so impactful for you?

2. Sheila said in the wake of her mother's death, even as she knew hope is a beautiful thing, she needed to *grieve*. How useful do you find "grieving" to be when it comes to acknowledging brokenness in our lives? How do you tend to honor the practice of grieving? What priorities or firsthand experiences help explain your tendencies?

3. What difference does it make for a person who is grieving to have a personal relationship with Christ? Along these lines, is there such a thing as grief that is useful, or hopeful, or good? Explain.

4. Sheila referred to the woman caught in adultery in John 8 and noted Jesus was at her side in her pain. In your deepest points of grief, where have *you* supposed God to be?

5. How did you react to Sheila's assertion that even though salvation doesn't remove the struggle from our lives, it delivers us inside that pain?

6. What are some things to which you have turned for deliverance instead of turning to God? What are some assumptions or fears that tend to keep you from looking heavenward in the midst of sorrow and grief?

Closing Prayer

Taking as much time as your group needs, have each member who feels comfortable complete the following prayer prompt as a way to close your discussion:

God, if I could have just one piece of the heavy brokenness I've been lugging around removed from this seemingly unbearable load, it would be . . .

Between-Sessions Personal Study

Session Two

Reflect on the content you've discussed this week by engaging in any or all of the following between-sessions personal studies. The time you invest will be well spent, so let God use it to draw you closer to Him. At your next meeting, share with your group any key points or insights that stood out to you as you spent this time with the Lord.

PART ONE: The Hard Stuff Is Indeed Hard

You can stuff it and deny it and try to pretty it up, but the truth remains: the hard stuff you're facing *is indeed hard*. You can't escape hardness in this fallen-world life. The next step to finding hope in the midst of your brokenness and pain—the one just after *accepting it is there*—is *acknowledging* its hardness. It's saying, "I feel this weight . . . I really do."

REVISIT YOUR EXPERIENCE

Take a few moments to revisit this week's teaching as it relates to your personal experience.

In session one, you noted the impact your present brokenness is having on your relationships, your finances, your emotional state, and more. Look back at pages 18–19 to see how you addressed each of the categories named, and then write in the space below which aspect feels "hardest" to work through today.

Why is it so difficult to focus on anything productive in life when you have a burden that feels hard—even impossible—to bear?

How well would you say you've managed your "hard" so far? How have you tried to fill the gaping hole that this situation has dug in your life?

White lilies. Cream tulips. Yellow roses.
Why do we make what's so sad look so pretty?
Why do we cover up our gaping holes?

—SHEILA WALSH

RECEIVE GOD'S TRUTH

Read the following Scripture passages and reflect on the related questions.

> So do not fear, for I am with you; do not be dismayed, for I am your God. I will strengthen you and help you; I will uphold you with my righteous right hand.
>
> (Isaiah 41:10)

This verse from Isaiah is intended to comfort those who love God, but it reveals a host of ugly truths regarding what life on earth truly is like. For instance, you can imply from the opening exhortation to "fear not" that you will, in fact, encounter some fearsome situations in this life. What other implications do you find in this verse? Note an implication beside each phrase listed below. Two examples have been provided for you.

Phrase	**Implication**
Do not fear	I will face some fear-filled situations.
I am with you	At times, I will feel alone.
Do not be dismayed	
I am your God	
I will strengthen you	
I will help you	
I will uphold you with my righteous right hand	

With the same goal of spotting implications, look at the following passages of Scripture. On the grid below, note the implications you discover as well as any firsthand experience you've had with each. An example has been provided for you.

Scripture	Implications	Firsthand Experience
Cast all your anxiety on him because he cares for you (1 Peter 5:7).	I will be anxious at times	I was anxious when I received the call from the doctor, but I remember that God cares for me.
I consider that our present sufferings are not worth comparing with the glory that will be revealed in us (Romans 8:18).		
You know that the testing of your faith produces perseverance. Let perseverance finish its work so that you may be mature and complete, not lacking anything (James 1:3–4).		
The LORD is a refuge for the oppressed, a stronghold in times of trouble. Those who know your name trust in you, for you, LORD, have never forsaken those who seek you (Psalm 9:9–10).		

(cont.)

Scripture	Implications	Firsthand Experience
Be strong and courageous. Do not be afraid; do not be discouraged, for the LORD your God will be with you wherever you go (Joshua 1:9).		
Weeping may stay for the night, but rejoicing comes in the morning (Psalm 30:5).		

Which of the implications and experiences stand out to you the most today? Why?

What emotions do you experience as you consider that this life is all but *guaranteed* to be hard?

What comfort can you gain from seeing that even before the formation of the world and the writing of His Word, God knew all the hard things you would face?

> Jesus went to the Mount of Olives. At dawn he appeared again in the temple courts, where all the people gathered around him, and he sat down to teach them. The teachers of the law and the Pharisees brought in a woman caught in adultery. They made her stand before the group and said to Jesus, "Teacher, this woman was caught in the act of adultery. In the Law Moses commanded us to stone such women. Now what do you say?" They were using this question as a trap, in order to have a basis for accusing him. But Jesus bent down and started to write on the ground with his finger.
>
> (John 8:1–6)

On the day in question, what was Jesus's intention for how His time with the people at the temple would be spent?

What was the intention of the scribes and Pharisees for how their time with Jesus would be spent?

How would you put words to the "hard" the woman caught in adultery felt? Which implications noted on the grid on pages 49–50 might she have most resonated with, and why?

> At this, those who heard began to go away one at a time, the older ones first, until only Jesus was left, with the woman still standing there.
>
> (John 8:9)

What had the scribes and Pharisees intended for the woman caught in adultery?

What does this verse reveal about what actually unfolded that day?

What is the significance of Jesus standing with this woman in the midst of perhaps the greatest humiliation and pain she'd ever known?

What encouragement does this scene offer you as you bear up under *your* hard thing?

The woman caught in adultery was dragged in front of the crowd and thrown in the dirt at the feet of Jesus. All eyes were on her, on her shame. The sin. The self-loathing. The judgment of the crowd. The embarrassment. The pain. But she wasn't alone in her mess, for there stood her Messiah.

—SHEILA WALSH

REORIENT YOUR HABITS AND HEART

As a means for bringing this theme to life—that of hardship indeed being "hard"—select one or more of the following to practice sometime today:

- Gather up some coins and, with your hand outstretched before you, palm facing the floor, stack one coin on top of another, naming each burden you feel. Notice how difficult it is to keep bearing those burdens on your own and how quickly the coins come tumbling down.
- Sit with the image of yourself wearing a weighted vest. All over the vest are tiny pockets where you can insert another weighted one-pound bag. Experiment with the idea of inserting a particular burden, such as "fretfulness over how I'm going to pay this month's rent." How do you feel after inserting that weight? What thoughts creep in once that weight is in place? Now, picture that weight being removed. What emotions bubble up as you feel the pounds come off your frame?

- Close your eyes and take ten deep breaths. With each inhale, focus on a particular aspect of your present brokenness. With each exhale, focus on that burden being lifted from you.
- Select a favorite worship song from a playlist and sing the chorus while focusing on the weight of your pain. Journal your findings on how challenging it is to engage in thoughts of hopefulness and hopelessness at the same time.

God had one son on earth without sin,
but never one without suffering.

—SAINT AUGUSTINE

PART TWO:
Jesus Is the Expert in "Hard"

If there is one person who understood just how difficult this life can be, it was Jesus Himself. During His three years of public ministry, He experienced direct attacks from His enemy, Satan. He experienced betrayal from His friend, Judas. He was taken captive by Roman guards. He was deserted by His closest friends. He was rejected by His own people. He was falsely accused by many witnesses. He was spat on, beat up, and mocked. And, ultimately, He was brutally crucified. It is for these reasons that the author of Hebrews tells us, "We do not have a high priest who is unable to empathize with our weaknesses, but we have one who has been tempted in every way, just as we are—yet he did not sin" (4:15). Jesus can *fully* relate to our suffering, and He is *uniquely* equipped to help.

REVISIT YOUR EXPERIENCE

Why do you think Jesus had to suffer so much during His earthly ministry? What was the purpose for His pain?

Why is it so easy to believe that *our suffering* is the hardest suffering of all?

What encouragement can you draw from the fact that Jesus suffered the deepest suffering possible and yet still did not sin?

RECEIVE GOD'S TRUTH

Read the following Scripture passages and reflect on the related questions.

> When they kept on questioning him, he straightened up and said to them, "Let any one of you who is without sin be the first to throw a stone at her." Again he stooped down and wrote on the ground.
>
> At this, those who heard began to go away one at a time, the older ones first, until only Jesus was left, with the woman still standing there. Jesus straightened up and asked her, "Woman, where are they? Has no one condemned you?"
>
> "No one, sir," she said.

> "Then neither do I condemn you," Jesus declared. "Go now and leave your life of sin."
>
> (John 8:7–11)

What happened in these verses to cause the scribes and Pharisees to drop their stones and leave the scene?

What emotions do you suppose the woman experienced as she observed her accusers each dropping a stone and walking away?

What was the significance of Jesus assuring this woman that she was no longer condemned?

What role do you think condemnation plays in the brokenness we experience in this life?

> For I am convinced that neither death nor life, neither angels nor demons, neither the present nor the future, nor any powers, neither height nor depth, nor anything else in all creation, will be able to separate us from the love of God that is in Christ Jesus our Lord.
>
> (Romans 8:38–39)

What nine things does Paul cite that are unable to keep us from the love of God?

Why did Paul choose such sweeping terms to describe how sturdy and steady God's love is toward us?

What is the connection between the condemnation our enemy would have us feel over the mess we find ourselves in and the love of God that is beating down every power and height and depth to reach us?

What challenges does a person mired in condemnation face in receiving this lavish love of God?

What challenges would you have to overcome to more fully let God's love in?

REORIENT YOUR HABITS AND HEART

To help reinforce this idea that Jesus is an expert in the "hard" we face in life, select one or more of the following to practice sometime today:

- Go outside and pick up a handful of rocks. Feel the weight of them in your hand as you picture the woman caught in adultery, who just knew she was about to be stoned. Picture yourself in her shoes, those rocks of accusation aimed at your legs, your body, your head. Now drop the rocks, one by one, naming each accuser as you do. *Shame. Anxiety. Self-loathing. Ridicule.* Assign a name to each and every one.
- In a quiet moment of solitude, read the journal entry Sheila quoted in this session's video segment aloud (see callout on the next page). Spend a few moments turning over key phrases in your mind. Which word or phrase can you carry with you throughout this day to serve as a reminder of hope and light and life?
- Memorize Romans 8:38–39. Each time you recite the verses, ask God to give you more of the "sureness" of which you speak.
- Swim in a pool, or imagine doing so. Think of Jesus's companionship as the water surrounding you. Focus on what weightlessness feels like. Sit with that image for a while.

I never knew you lived so close to the floor, but every time I am bowed down, crushed by this weight of grief, I feel your hand on my head, your breath on my cheek, your tears on my neck. You never tell me to pull myself together, to stem the flow of many tears. You simply stay by my side for as long as it takes, so close to the floor.

—SHEILA WALSH

PART THREE:
Deliverance Is at Hand

The logical question after admitting the hardness of your situation is, "Where, then, can I find relief?" In other words, now that you've acknowledged you have this weight pressing down on your chest, is there anyone anywhere who would be kind enough to take it from you? The good news is that this "expert in hard," our Messiah, Jesus, stands ready to lift that weight. The challenge in receiving His assistance is that you must set all other fixes aside.

REVISIT YOUR EXPERIENCE

Sheila acknowledged that when it comes to dealing with suffering and pain, her *modus operandi* is to begin erecting a protective wall. In her book *In the Middle of the Mess*, she writes:

> We all know that pain is part of life, but when too much of it happens all at once—when it happens too early in life or when we feel helpless to combat it—the pain can make us believe we don't want to go on. It's why we build a secret

place inside ourselves where we can hang out. The pain might follow us there, but we believe it can't hurt us as much if it's walled up. And we falsely think that the world can't see it either.

What types of "walls" do you generally hide behind when the pain of life feels too weighty to bear? The wall of "all-rightness," where you deny that anything is wrong? The wall of control? Of distraction? Of isolation? Of rage? Explain.

Our huffing and puffing to impress God, our scrambling for brownie points, our thrashing about trying to fix ourselves while hiding our pettiness and wallowing in guilt are nauseating to God and are a flat-out denial of the gospel of grace.

—BRENNAN MANNING

RECEIVE GOD'S TRUTH

Read the following Scripture passages and reflect on the related questions.

> Some time later God tested Abraham. He said to him, "Abraham!"
>
> "Here I am," he replied.
>
> Then God said, "Take your son, your only son, whom you love—Isaac—and go to the region of Moriah. Sacrifice him there as a burnt offering on a mountain I will show you."

Early the next morning Abraham got up and loaded his donkey. He took with him two of his servants and his son Isaac. When he had cut enough wood for the burnt offering, he set out for the place God had told him about. On the third day Abraham looked up and saw the place in the distance. He said to his servants, "Stay here with the donkey while I and the boy go over there. We will worship and then we will come back to you."

Abraham took the wood for the burnt offering and placed it on his son Isaac, and he himself carried the fire and the knife. As the two of them went on together, Isaac spoke up and said to his father Abraham, "Father?"

"Yes, my son?" Abraham replied.

"The fire and wood are here," Isaac said, "but where is the lamb for the burnt offering?"

Abraham answered, "God himself will provide the lamb for the burnt offering, my son." And the two of them went on together.

When they reached the place God had told him about, Abraham built an altar there and arranged the wood on it. He bound his son Isaac and laid him on the altar, on top of the wood. Then he reached out his hand and took the knife to slay his son. But the angel of the Lord called out to him from heaven, "Abraham! Abraham!"

"Here I am," he replied.

"Do not lay a hand on the boy," he said. "Do not do anything to him. Now I know that you fear God, because you have not withheld from me your son, your only son."

Abraham looked up and there in a thicket he saw a ram caught by its horns. He went over and took the ram and sacrificed it as a burnt offering instead of his son. So Abraham called that place The Lord Will Provide. And to this day it is said, "On the mountain of the Lord it will be provided."

The angel of the Lord called to Abraham from heaven a second time and said, "I swear by myself, declares the Lord, that because you have done this and have not withheld your son, your only son, I will surely bless you and make your descendants as numerous as the stars in the sky and as the sand on the seashore. Your descendants will take possession of the cities of their enemies, and through your offspring all nations on earth will be blessed, because you have obeyed me."

(Genesis 22:1–18)

This scene opens with a clear command from God to Abraham. What was that command?

Why did God make such a request of Abraham—a man who had been incredibly faithful to Him?

What was Abraham's reaction to God's request?

What was Abraham's rationale for responding to God in this way? Select any that apply from the list below:

- ☐ He knew God could be trusted.
- ☐ He knew God saw his situation.
- ☐ He knew God loved him.
- ☐ He knew God loved Isaac.
- ☐ He knew God would provide a way out.
- ☐ He knew God would keep His promise to protect him.
- ☐ He knew God had good things in store for him.
- ☐ He knew God had good things in store for Isaac.
- ☐ He knew God could see the bigger picture here.

How is this scene between the heavenly Father, God, and an earthly father, Abraham, a picture of salvation not necessarily removing the struggle but instead delivering us inside the struggle?

What would it look like for you to be delivered "inside your struggle"?

No one ever told me that grief felt so like fear.

—C. S. LEWIS

REORIENT YOUR HABITS AND HEART

In order for Abraham to fix his eyes on his heavenly Father and trust God would take him out of this mess, he had to grieve *toward God,* not away from God. He had to bring his loss to the Lord. This is what "good grief" accomplishes: it draws us near to the heart of God. As Sheila writes in *In the Middle of the Mess*, "What happened with Abraham and Isaac on Mount Moriah all those years ago wasn't a cruel test; it was the very embodiment of the promise of deliverance. And my deliverance—our deliverance—was made possible by the Lamb of God."

What "other solutions" do you suppose Abraham had to set aside to look to God alone to get him out of the mess he was in?

As you look at the effect of the grief you carry today, do you sense it leading you closer to your heavenly Father or farther and farther away? Explain.

What concerns do you have about trusting God fully to deliver you from your suffering and pain?

"Blessed are those who mourn, for they shall be comforted."

—JESUS (MATTHEW 5:4)

PRACTICING THE DISCIPLINE OF GOOD GRIEF

It may seem strange to view grief as a discipline, but indeed it is. The process of grieving says to our pain, "I won't merely acknowledge your presence and move forward; I will sit with you here for a while. I will weigh your impact on my heart and my life. I will assess what your reality means." In the same way the scale at the gym gives you a concrete number from which to work as you seek to lose weight, the process of grieving reveals just how deep this mess is that you've been muddling through all this time.

During this session's video segment, Sheila described the "weight" of her pain this way: "Mum's death shook me to my core. She'd always been such a tower of strength in my life—quiet, rock-solid strength. She loved me on my good days and on my bad. It's what moms do. Now she was gone, and I felt . . . *little*." This was grief, in all its rawness. But God wouldn't leave Sheila there in her grief.

1. Allow Yourself to Feel the Grief

Can you relate to this *sense of smallness* Sheila describes—that feeling of fragility that suffering seems always to usher in? Go ahead and sit with those feelings, acknowledging the weight of the weightiest things in your life. Quiet your mind and your voice, and turn your thoughts toward your pain. What is your *experience* of suffering just now? You might form a picture in your mind's eye, a metaphor, to describe how things feel for you. A ship tossed about an open sea, perhaps? A walk on unstable footing, through a dark and misty forest? That terrible feeling of breathlessness when the air gets knocked out of your chest? Focus on a scenario of your own imagining and allow the feelings it evokes to wash over you like a wave.

2. Picture Jesus as Your Deliverer

After a few minutes, release this scenario from your mind. Sit in a comfortable position and open your hands. Picture Jesus entering the room, approaching you, and placing a beautifully wrapped gift in your hands. "I want to show you things you cannot yet perceive," He says. "I want to bring beauty from the ashes you've held. This gift I'm giving you is greater perspective. Will you trust me enough to open it up?" Notice that as you hold the gift Jesus has handed you, you can't hold anything else. All the weight you were hanging onto, all the burdens you'd been hoisting up with your hands . . . it all has fallen away as you cling to this divinely placed gift.

3. Seek God's Perspective

As you conclude your time in this session, sit with this question a few moments: *Am I ready for the greater perspective that God's insight always brings?* What risks might you face if you say yes? What reward might you miss out on for saying no? Ponder these ideas for as long as you need before writing a letter to your heavenly Father, telling Him all that is on your heart. (Use the space provided on page 66.)

Before the next meeting, read chapters 5 and 6 of *In the Middle of the Mess*.

Session Three

Brokenness Is Loud

Confident Confession

To confess your sins to God is not to tell God anything God doesn't already know. Until you confess them, however, they are the abyss between you. When you confess them to God, they become the Golden Gate Bridge.

Frederick Buechner

Session Overview

So many opinions exist regarding how we "should" respond to suffering and pain. Experts, authors, spouses, bosses, neighbors, colleagues, and friends—who doesn't have a perspective, and one they feel passionately about?

In Session 2, we concluded with an invitation to look to God for our deliverance, and to look to Him alone. The reason we did this is because until we have adopted God's perspective on our pain, we can't rightly sort through others' explanations and well-meaning advice. And so, tucked here between our grief (Session 2), and our willingness to invite others into our journey (Session 4), is this prompting to come to the Lord.

As you go through this session today, look for ways to knock on His door, with your grief humbly in hand, and say, "Father, *please* take this from me."

Opening Thoughts

Take one to two minutes to open your time together with prayer. Then, have each group member answer the following questions before watching the video segment:

What is a highlight from your between-sessions learning that you would like to share with the group?

What's the worst piece of advice you've ever received—regarding personal development, parenting, finances, job interviews, or anything else? What's the best piece of advice you've ever received?

Video: Brokenness Is Loud (20 MINUTES)

Play the video for Session 3. Use the following prompts to record your thoughts as you watch.

VIDEO NOTES

A needed getaway

A little thing feels big to the brokenhearted

Job, a man blameless in God's sight

Job's cry: "Obliterate the day I was born! Blank out the night I was conceived!"

Ignorant cruelty from well-meaning friends

Job's boldest and bravest decision

Why we stuff our anger and pain

The One who saves the crushed in spirit

"To release, to let slack, to let go"

Listening for that still, small voice

Group Discussion

Spend the balance of your group time answering as many of the following questions as you have time and energy for, being sure to give equal opportunity for each member to share.

1. Based on the notes you wrote down during this session's video segment, what phrase, story, or big idea do you hope to apply to your life?

2. Sheila told of the frustration she experienced during her getaway to the Gulf of Mexico, when the world was seemingly conspiring against her. When have you had a similar experience, where it seemed the world was trying to push you over sanity's edge? Describe the situation for your group.

3. As you consider your current circumstances—your present area of brokenness and pain—which season of Job's story do you most resonate with, and why? Select one from the list that begins below, and then explain your thoughts to your group.

   - ☐ Utter shock from heartbreak and loss
   - ☐ Disillusionment over all that once was

- ☐ Anger regarding the seeming punishment of deep pain
- ☐ Humiliation/sober-mindedness upon being reminded of God's presence and strength
- ☐ Relief over realizing God was with you all along
- ☐ Regained fulfillment as God restores you to a better place than you inhabited before

4. As Sheila noted, many people in Job's life offered opinions about why he was suffering as well as "helpful advice" for how to better understand his pain. What input have you received as you've endured your struggles? How do you know which advice to brush aside and which advice to take?

5. How do you react to Sheila's assertion that the primary reason you and I don't more readily come to God with our pain and our protests is that we don't want to "seem ungodly"? What might be construed as "ungodly" about venting to the Lord?

6. Sheila cited the words of Psalm 46:10 as God's invitation for her to release whatever was binding her and find solace there in Him. What do you think a Christ follower can know in stillness with God that cannot be known any other way?

Closing Prayer

Taking as much time as your group needs, have each member who feels comfortable complete either of the following prayer prompts as a way to close your discussion:

God, when I consider coming before you, with all of the aspects and nuances and details of my present suffering there on my lips, I feel . . .

Lord, if there is one thing I would ask of you as I muster the courage to confess my whole truth, it would be . . .

Between-Sessions Personal Study

Session Three

Reflect on the content you've discussed this week by engaging in any or all of the following between-sessions personal studies. The time you invest will be well spent, so let God use it to draw you closer to Him. At your next meeting, share with your group any key points or insights that stood out to you as you spent this time with the Lord.

PART ONE:
Loudness Doesn't Equal Rightness

The danger of listening to "other opinions"—whether shouted from within your own mind or from the mouths of well-meaning friends—is that until you have heard from God directly, you are like a ship adrift on the turbulent sea. Any whim or wind can sway you; any storm can take you down. But in the face of opinions that are so plentiful, and "wisdom" that is so loud, can you really be expected to stay in your pain, avoiding this advice that could actually help? What is the alternative available to you? Or maybe there's no real alternative at all?

REVISIT YOUR EXPERIENCE

Sheila relates that after her mother's death, she experienced an onslaught of "well-meaning advice" courtesy of her Facebook page. One comment in particular cut her to the core: "Just think how God is going to use this next part of your story for His glory. Hallelujah! Our pain is His purpose." Certainly, Scripture supports the idea that God brings beauty from ashes and orchestrates purposeful outputs from our pain. But to receive such input at that time, with her loss still so fresh, just added more pain, measure upon measure.

Similarly, during her ill-fated trip to the Gulf of Mexico, Sheila fell prey to lies from the enemy and from her own mind—lies of incrimination, of hopelessness, of doom.

You're never going to feel happy again.
Your life is a total waste.
This time away won't solve anything.
You're doomed, Sheila—it's time you realized that.

On and on the lies went, sending her spiraling further down.

Can you relate to this unfortunate tendency of receiving unhelpful input when you're deeply in pain? When you think of the unhelpful input you've believed along the way, what memories or recollections come to mind? Where did the advice come from—your own self-talk? Satan? a friend? Why were the words so unhelpful to you?

Spend some time responding to the prompts below regarding three "scenes" from the pain you've known, noting the circumstances you were dealing with, the input you received, and the effect it had on your heart, spirit, and mind.

Scene One

When I walked through . . .

I remember being told that . . .

The effect it had on me was . . .

Scene Two

When I walked through . . .

I remember being told that . . .

The effect it had on me was . . .

Scene Three

When I walked through . . .

I remember being told that . . .

The effect it had on me was . . .

Before moving on, take another look at the scenes you cited above. Why does "helpful input" seem so decidedly unhelpful when we're in the depths of our agony and pain?

The enemy loves to use our brokenness to remind us how very vulnerable we are. He loves to brag about how much damage has been done. He loves to make us believe that nothing has changed.

—SHEILA WALSH

RECEIVE GOD'S TRUTH

Read the following Scripture passages and reflect on the related questions.

> After this, Job opened his mouth and cursed the day of his birth. He said:
>
> "May the day of my birth perish,
>   and the night that said, 'A boy is conceived!'
> That day—may it turn to darkness;
>   may God above not care about it;
>   may no light shine on it.
> May gloom and utter darkness claim it once more;
>   may a cloud settle over it;
>   may blackness overwhelm it.
> That night—may thick darkness seize it;
>   may it not be included among the days of the year

nor be entered in any of the months.
May that night be barren;
may no shout of joy be heard in it.
May those who curse days curse that day,
those who are ready to rouse Leviathan.
May its morning stars become dark;
may it wait for daylight in vain
and not see the first rays of dawn,
for it did not shut the doors of the womb on me
to hide trouble from my eyes."

(Job 3:1–10)

Job spoke these words just after Satan pillaged his life, taking his children's lives, his livestock, his fortune, his health, and his hope. In what ways can you relate to Job responding to these events with such outrage and desperation?

How do you think you would have responded if Job's circumstances had come to you?

How would you describe Job's self-talk in these verses? When have you fallen prey to making disparaging remarks to yourself?

Why does hope seem so elusive whenever suffering has come our way? Why can't we remember in darkness what we were certain of in the light?

Then Eliphaz the Temanite replied . . .

"As I have observed, those who plow evil
and those who sow trouble reap it.
At the breath of God they perish;
at the blast of his anger they are no more.
The lions may roar and growl,
yet the teeth of the great lions are broken.
The lion perishes for lack of prey,
and the cubs of the lioness are scattered."

(Job 4:1, 8–11)

Job's own self-talk wasn't the only negative input he received before he determined to look to God for relief. The first friend he heard was Eliphaz, who is quoted in the passage above. What rationale for Job's suffering did Eliphaz provide his friend?

What consequences would you imagine Job would have faced if he believed only the innocent prosper, as Eliphaz stated?

Then Bildad the Shuhite replied:

"How long will you say such things?
Your words are a blustering wind.

Does God pervert justice?
    Does the Almighty pervert what is right?
When your children sinned against him,
    he gave them over to the penalty of their sin.
But if you will seek God earnestly
    and plead with the Almighty,
if you are pure and upright,
    even now he will rouse himself on your behalf
    and restore you to your prosperous state.
Your beginnings will seem humble,
    so prosperous will your future be."

(Job 8:1–7)

What advice did Bildad have regarding why Job was suffering?

What impact do you suppose Bildad's idea had on Job—that Job's suffering was a direct result of his children having sinned?

Then Zophar the Naamathite replied:

"Are all these words to go unanswered?
    Is this talker to be vindicated?
Will your idle talk reduce others to silence?
    Will no one rebuke you when you mock?
You say to God, 'My beliefs are flawless
    and I am pure in your sight.'
Oh, how I wish that God would speak,
    that he would open his lips against you

and disclose to you the secrets of wisdom,
for true wisdom has two sides.
Know this: God has even forgotten some of your sin."

(Job 11:2–6)

What was Zophar essentially saying to Job?

How would you feel if a friend visited you during your time of deepest pain and grief and said that you deserved worse than the suffering you'd received?

[Job said,]

"But where can wisdom be found?
Where does understanding dwell?
No mortal comprehends its worth;
it cannot be found in the land of the living.
The deep says, 'It is not in me';
the sea says, 'It is not with me.'"

(Job 28:12–14)

What do you think prompted Job to ask where wisdom could be found?

Read Jeremiah 33:2–4. What does God promise in this passage? What does this say about how Job could have received wisdom in his situation?

Would you have accepted God's invitation if you were in Job's situation? Why or why not? What would you have risked to "call to Him," and what might you have gained?

When the pain is freshest, the words should be fewest.

—BARBARA JOHNSON

REORIENT YOUR HABITS AND HEART

To further explore this theme regarding the loud opinions of our suffering not necessarily being right, select one or more of the following to practice sometime today:

- List some occasions when, in your pain and confusion, you have run to the advice of others or have caved to the lies of the enemy instead of first going to your heavenly Father and giving voice to His will and His ways.
- If you live in a city, head outside and stand in the midst of the noise. Take in the jackhammers, the blaring horns, the many different conversations, the sounds of industry at work. If you live in a quieter setting, play some rapid-paced music and perhaps turn the volume up louder than may be wise. Consider for a few moments how challenging it is to think clearly and feel steady with this noise around you.

- Sit in a position that is not typical for you. For a full minute, hold this position while you consider the emotional tornado you find yourself in whenever you fail to bring your pain first to God.
- Grab a pad of sticky notes. On each, write one of the lies that Satan has hissed at you during the course of your life. Rip or cut up the notes and throw them into the trash. Then write out a prayer to God declaring your readiness to receive His truth.

Job was done. He was in full-on agony of soul. And just as you and I experience, in those moments there's no good to be found.

—SHEILA WALSH

PART TWO:
Where All Wisdom Is Found

Fortunately for Job—and for you!—there is wisdom to be found. You don't have to subject yourself to half-baked truths or outright lies spoken by Satan or well-meaning friends. When you're hip-deep in pain and confusion, you can do just as Jeremiah instructed you to do: call on God, knowing that He will answer and show you things you did not know.

REVISIT YOUR EXPERIENCE

What is your working definition of *wisdom*? What influences have shaped your thoughts?

If you were to imagine wisdom as a person (throughout Proverbs, it is referred to as "she"), what human characteristics would this person possess?

Think of a time when you opted for wisdom. How did it feel to do something wise?

When have you been spared unnecessary suffering as a result of walking in wisdom's ways?

RECEIVE GOD'S TRUTH

Read the following Scripture passages and reflect on the related questions.

> If any of you lacks wisdom, you should ask God, who gives generously to all without finding fault, and it will be given to you.
>
> (James 1:5)

How does James describe God's dispensing of wisdom to those who ask?

Why isn't God more guarded in offering His wisdom to those who ask?

What are some qualifications that God *could* have placed on dispensing wisdom? Note your ideas in the space below.

God could have offered wisdom only to those who . . .

> The fear of the Lord is the beginning of knowledge, but fools despise wisdom and instruction.
>
> (Proverbs 1:7)

What type of "fear" is Solomon, the author of Proverbs, referring to when he says the "fear" of the Lord is the beginning of all knowledge?

When have you been "foolish," as defined by this verse?

What kept you from pursuing wisdom during that season of life?

Based on the sequence depicted in this verse—that fearing the Lord comes before knowledge can be grasped—how well do you believe you are "choosing wisdom" in the midst of your present pain?

What fears or insecurities do you have regarding giving yourself over fully to wisdom's ways?

REORIENT YOUR HABITS AND HEART

To help reinforce this theme about where all true wisdom is found, select one or more of the following to practice sometime today:

- In a moment of solitude, ask yourself the question, "If God's wisdom is so readily available to me, then why am I not more willing to passionately pursue it?" Journal the answers that come to mind.
- Ask the Lord for insight regarding any ways in which you're presently "playing the fool." Bring these issues before Him in prayer, asking Him to open you up to change.
- Read the words to the hymn, "Where Can One Look for Wisdom" (below). Sit for a few minutes with the idea that God understands the "pathway." What do these words mean to you, given the present struggle you're facing?

Where can one look for wisdom?
Where understanding find?
Man does not grasp its value—
More than can be mined.
It can't be bought with finest gold,
Silver, or jewels so rare.
Priced far beyond all rubies,
Nothing can compare.

Where then does wisdom come from?
Where understanding dwell?
God comprehends the pathway,
He alone knows well.
He views the ends of all the earth;
He sees the world He formed.
He has established wisdom,
Tested and confirmed.

(cont.)

Fear of the Lord is wisdom;
Seek it and you will find.
Cry out for understanding;
Let it fill your mind.
Search as for hidden treasure;
Look for it every day.
This is the path to wisdom;
Follow all the way.

—Lowell Mason, "Where Can One Look for Wisdom" (1864)

PART THREE:
What Wise People Do

Down through the ages, there are several things all wise people do: slow their pace, seek their Creator, and persist until they receive wisdom from Him. "Be still, and know that I am God," the psalmist wrote on God's behalf in Psalm 46:10. And while that calling is a high one to anyone living in today's modern world, the rewards to be found there are sweet.

REVISIT YOUR EXPERIENCE

What does it mean to truly "be still" and know that "God is God"?

When have you experienced a time of knowing, there from a quieted position, that God truly is God?

What keeps you from practicing this stillness more often than you do?

What would it mean for you to "know that God is God" in the middle of the mess you find yourself in right now?

It's a discipline to push in, to press on into His presence. But the truth is, He is always waiting for us. "I'm here," He says. "I know. I care."

SHEILA WALSH

RECEIVE GOD'S TRUTH

Read the following Scripture passages and reflect on the related questions.

[Job said,]

"I made a covenant with my eyes
not to look lustfully at a young woman.
For what is our lot from God above,
our heritage from the Almighty on high?
Is it not ruin for the wicked,

disaster for those who do wrong?
Does he not see my ways
and count my every step?

"If I have walked with falsehood
or my foot has hurried after deceit—
let God weigh me in honest scales
and he will know that I am blameless—
if my steps have turned from the path,
if my heart has been led by my eyes,
or if my hands have been defiled,
then may others eat what I have sown,
and may my crops be uprooted.

"If my heart has been enticed by a woman,
or if I have lurked at my neighbor's door,
then may my wife grind another man's grain,
and may other men sleep with her.
For that would have been wicked,
a sin to be judged.
It is a fire that burns to Destruction;
it would have uprooted my harvest.

"If I have denied justice to any of my servants,
whether male or female,
when they had a grievance against me,
what will I do when God confronts me?
What will I answer when called to account?
Did not he who made me in the womb make them?
Did not the same one form us both within our mothers?

"If I have denied the desires of the poor
or let the eyes of the widow grow weary,

if I have kept my bread to myself,
    not sharing it with the fatherless—
but from my youth I reared them as a father would,
    and from my birth I guided the widow—
if I have seen anyone perishing for lack of clothing,
    or the needy without garments,
and their hearts did not bless me
    for warming them with the fleece from my sheep,
if I have raised my hand against the fatherless,
    knowing that I had influence in court,
then let my arm fall from the shoulder,
    let it be broken off at the joint.
For I dreaded destruction from God,
    and for fear of his splendor I could not do such things.

"If I have put my trust in gold
    or said to pure gold, 'You are my security,'
if I have rejoiced over my great wealth,
    the fortune my hands had gained,
if I have regarded the sun in its radiance
    or the moon moving in splendor,
so that my heart was secretly enticed
    and my hand offered them a kiss of homage,
then these also would be sins to be judged,
    for I would have been unfaithful to God on high.

"If I have rejoiced at my enemy's misfortune
    or gloated over the trouble that came to him—
I have not allowed my mouth to sin
    by invoking a curse against their life—
if those of my household have never said,
    'Who has not been filled with Job's meat?'—
but no stranger had to spend the night in the street,

for my door was always open to the traveler—
if I have concealed my sin as people do,
by hiding my guilt in my heart
because I so feared the crowd
and so dreaded the contempt of the clans
that I kept silent and would not go outside—

("Oh, that I had someone to hear me!
I sign now my defense—let the Almighty answer me;
let my accuser put his indictment in writing.
Surely I would wear it on my shoulder,
I would put it on like a crown.
I would give him an account of my every step;
I would present it to him as to a ruler.)—

"if my land cries out against me
and all its furrows are wet with tears,
if I have devoured its yield without payment
or broken the spirit of its tenants,
then let briers come up instead of wheat
and stinkweed instead of barley."

(Job 31:1–40)

What are the seven big "if" statements Job chooses to present to God? Note them in your own words in the space below.

- If I have walked . . . (verses 5–8)

- If my heart . . . (verses 9–12)

- If I have denied . . . (verses 13–15)

- If I have denied . . . (verses 16–23)

- If I have put . . . (verses 24–28)

- If I have rejoiced . . . (verses 29–34)

- If my land . . . (verses 38–40)

In essence, what was Job saying in his lengthy discourse to God?

What concerns do you imagine Job had to overcome to bring his truth before God?

How do you imagine Job must have felt after releasing his (quite full!) burden to God?

Then the Lord spoke to Job out of the storm. He said:

"Who is this that obscures my plans
with words without knowledge?
Brace yourself like a man;
I will question you,
and you shall answer me.

"Where were you when I laid the earth's foundation?
Tell me, if you understand.
Who marked off its dimensions? Surely you know!
Who stretched a measuring line across it?
On what were its footings set,
or who laid its cornerstone—
while the morning stars sang together
and all the angels shouted for joy?

"Who shut up the sea behind doors
when it burst forth from the womb,
when I made the clouds its garment
and wrapped it in thick darkness,
when I fixed limits for it
and set its doors and bars in place,
when I said, 'This far you may come and no farther;
here is where your proud waves halt'?"

(Job 38:1–11)

Clearly, the Lord had something to say in response to Job protesting the justness of his suffering and pain. The preceding passage is but a portion of that reply, but given the tone you detect, what was God trying to show to Job?

What emotions do you suspect Job felt upon receiving the Lord's reply?

How would you imagine Job ranking his decision to shoot straight with God on his "worth-it" scale?

Despite God's strong response to Job's protests, what comfort might Job have taken in being reminded of God's power and prominence in the earth?

Earlier, we explored how knowledge begins with the "fear of the LORD" (Proverbs 1:7). It is for good reason we fear Him, for from Him comes every good thing. It was God, alone, who laid the earth's foundation. It was God, alone, who determined its measurements. It was God, alone, who placed its cornerstone. It was God, alone, who shut in the sea, saying, "Here is where your proud waves halt" (Job 38:11).

There is nothing good in all of the earth, in fact, that didn't come from the good hand of God. And there is no hope for us, His children on earth, apart from our intimate relationship with Him. Here, in response to Job, we get the feeling that God's posture was, "Come! Tell me everything you are feeling. Tell me exactly why you're so upset over this latest round of pain you've been made to endure. I will listen patiently as you lay it all out. And then I will remind you in no uncertain terms why your petitions are safe with me."

God would not be mocked, but He would not be manhandled either. He is good—but He remains God. Surely Job felt the full weight of this truth. It is because of God's power and preeminence that we can find our safety and surety in Him.

When you consider God in light of these readings, which of the following roles most readily come to mind? Check any that apply.

- ☐ God is a distant ruler.
- ☐ God is a true deliverer.
- ☐ God is a best friend.
- ☐ God is a worthy confidant.
- ☐ God is a fearsome force.
- ☐ God is a sheltering tree.
- ☐ God is a jovial relative.
- ☐ God is a pious priest.
- ☐ God is a safe harbor.
- ☐ God is a loving father.
- ☐ God is a benevolent dictator.
- ☐ God is ________________.

For Sheila, coming to the realization that the almighty, all-powerful, all-knowing, all-present God was also the most tender of confidants—the safest of shelters in times of storm—was a truly momentous thing. In her book *In the Middle of the Mess*, she writes:

> I recalled carrying Christian through the Miami airport late one night. He must have been about eighteen months old. It had been a very long day, and he whispered in my ear, "Mommy, I've wet myself. Will you cover me?" I wrapped my coat around him and held him tight. He never saw the tears running down my face for the gift he'd just given me. What he'd said to me was, "I trust you, Mom. You are my safe place."
>
> That's the way it should be for children. For God's children too. But can we trust that God wants to cover our shame, our pain? When you believe that your mom or dad will cover you, then it's easier, more natural, to believe that God will cover you too. But when you believe that your parents can't or won't, you learn to cover yourself. Covering myself worked for me . . . until it didn't anymore. Because when the clods of damp earth hit my mum's casket, I wanted to wail. I felt vulnerable, exposed, and uncovered.
>
> Months after my mum's death, after the horrid trip to the beach, and while I was carrying so much pain, God reminded me of that moment with Christian.
>
> "I am your Covering," He said.
>
> "I am your Safe Place."
>
> "I am."
>
> "Tell Me everything."

And so, with no small amount of trepidation, she did.

REORIENT YOUR HABITS AND HEART

To confirm this idea of God being your safe place, a sure foundation, the One who alone possesses power to protect you from the pain you feel, gather up a warm blanket and your Bible and head to a quiet place where you can sit uninterrupted for a half hour or so. Once you are comfortable, open your Bible to Psalm 46 (also shown below). Read the words of these verses aloud, with emphasis on each reference to God. Why is God a trustworthy confidant? In what ways is He uniquely able to absorb our protests of pain? How would your circumstances seem different if you truly believed that God's presence and power and compassion covered every inch of your life?

God is our refuge and strength,
  an ever-present help in trouble.
Therefore we will not fear, though the earth give way
  and the mountains fall into the heart of the sea,
though its waters roar and foam
  and the mountains quake with their surging.

There is a river whose streams make glad the city of God,
  the holy place where the Most High dwells.
God is within her, she will not fall;
  God will help her at break of day.
Nations are in uproar, kingdoms fall;
  he lifts his voice, the earth melts.

The LORD Almighty is with us;
  the God of Jacob is our fortress.
Come and see what the LORD has done,
  the desolations he has brought on the earth.
He makes wars cease
  to the ends of the earth.
He breaks the bow and shatters the spear;

(cont.)

he burns the shields with fire.
He says, "Be still, and know that I am God;
I will be exalted among the nations,
I will be exalted in the earth."
The LORD Almighty is with us;
the God of Jacob is our fortress.

(PSALM 46:1–11)

PRACTICING THE DISCIPLINE OF HONEST CONFESSION

Theologian Frederick Buechner once compared confession to God with the Golden Gate Bridge, which spans the length of our suffering and sin. This bridge is paved by perspective—and divine perspective at that. Job received this perspective and fell silent in awe after being reminded of God's majesty and unparalleled power. "How can I reply to you?" he asked rhetorically in Job 40:4. "I put my hand over my mouth." So it is that as you shift your gaze from the brokenness that burdens you to the Ultimate Burden-Bearer Himself, you step over to God's side of the bridge. You begin to see your sorrowful state from His vast point of view.

If you long for broader perspective—for your eyes to be lifted from your troubles and pain—then it is time to come to the Lord in a posture of confession. It is time to lay your great burden down. Come to Him, your all-encompassing covering. Come, and speak your truth.

1. Turn Your Attention to God

To begin, remember who it is you're coming before. He is the all-powerful, all-knowing One, but He is also the One who formed you and called you and loves you with an everlasting love. Below and continuing on the next two pages, you'll find lyrics to Sheila's song "Throne of Grace." Read the phrases one at a time to prepare your mind and heart for coming to the Lord in prayer.

Come to the Throne of Grace
Don't be afraid
I won't turn you away

Just let Me into your heart
And My love will wash your tears away

I know you
I know you completely
And on your darkest journey
I have been with you

All the weight of guilt and shame
You carry on your shoulders
It's time to hand it over
And let it go

Come to the Throne of Grace
Don't be afraid
I won't turn you away
Just let Me into your heart
And My love will wash your tears away

I can hear the silent tears
Above the noise and laughter
The things you're running after
Will let you down

So here I stand before you now
With arms of love to hold you
Let my grace enfold you
And come to me . . .
Run to me!

Come to the Throne of Grace
Don't be afraid
I won't turn you away

Just let Me into your heart
And My love will wash your tears away . . .

Come . . .
Just come . . .
Come . . .

2. Raise Your Voice

Next, speak your truth aloud. As uncomfortable as this may feel for you, leave no part of your pain unsaid. Tell God the whole truth—the truth as you see it, anyway. Agree with Him that this is what is real for you today. Without equivocation, speak.

3. Listen for God's Reply

Listen carefully to what God is saying to you in the wake of confessing your reality to Him. What truth is He reminding you of? What action is He asking you to take? Use the page provided to log the thoughts and promptings that come to mind.

Before the next meeting, read chapters 7 and 8 of *In the Middle of the Mess.*

Session Four

Brokenness Is to Be Shared

Safe Community of Truth-Tellers

Therefore, confess your sins to one another and pray for one another, that you may be healed. The prayer of a righteous person has great power as it is working.

JAMES 5:16 ESV

Session Overview

It may be tempting—once we discover just how faithful God is to listen to our confessions, absorb our frustrations, and right the errant perspectives we've held—to want to stay put there forever in the warmth and certainty of His embrace. "It's just me and Jesus!" we declare in our heart, "Jesus is all I need!" And yet we need only glance at our heavenly Father's subtle shake of the head to grasp His response: *Not so fast . . .*

It is true that confession to God is necessary, as it builds that bridge from our perspective to God's. But it is not the only confession we need. Confession is also to occur to *one another*. We are to entrust our truth to others walking along this broken way.

In this session, we will come to understand God's "community" priority. We will explore the risks and the rewards of vulnerability. And we will practice appropriate person-to-person confession toward the goal of "being healed."

Opening Thoughts

Take one to two minutes to open your time together with prayer. Then, have each group member answer the following questions before watching the video segment:

What is a highlight from your between-sessions learning that you would like to share with the group?

What words, images, emotions, assumptions, or expectations come to mind when you hear the word *vulnerability*? When was the last time you were "vulnerable" with another person? Describe the occasion for your group.

Video: Brokenness Is to Be Shared (21 MINUTES)

Play the video for Session 4. Use the following prompts to record your thoughts as you watch.

VIDEO NOTES

Sheila's mom's vulnerable example

On falling off of one's shelf

"I've got Jesus, and that's all I need"

Jesus's highest high . . . and lowest low

What Jesus did on the night before His death

To know that someone sees our pain

"Engage! Show up! Invite someone else in!"

The natural outpouring of time spent in God's presence

"When you want to run away, run here"

On being stirred to love and good works

Brokenness as our common denominator

Group Discussion

Spend the balance of your group time answering as many of the following questions as you have time and energy for, being sure to give equal opportunity for each member to share.

1. What word or phrase from this session's video segment did you make sure to write down? What really stood out to you, and why?

2. Sheila described her journey as it relates to valuing *community* as a part of God's healing plan. Along the same lines, what has your journey looked like? In what ways have you prized the others-centeredness that God encourages? In what ways is this still an area of growth for you? Share your thoughts and observations with your group.

3. When have you known a magnificent sense of comfort and peace as a result of "letting someone else into" your pain, and how has that experience deepened your resolve not to go it alone in life?

4. On the flip side of that coin, when have you been stung by sharing your truth with another person? Without divulging any details, what challenges did the turn of events present for you? What emotions proved challenging to overcome?

5. Sheila said that in regard to *when* you should be vulnerable with others, a good rule of thumb is to confide in others only what you've first confided in God. How faithful have you been throughout your life to follow such a sequence?

6. What pain, awkwardness, or ill-advised conversations might you have avoided if you had followed this plan better? Explain.

Closing Prayer

Taking as much time as your group needs, have each member who feels comfortable complete the following prayer prompt as a way to close your discussion:

God, when it comes to inviting others into my suffering so they can help me bear the load, I want to acknowledge before you and before my friends that . . .

Between-Sessions Personal Study

Session Four

Reflect on the content you've discussed this week by engaging in any or all of the following between-sessions personal studies. The time you invest will be well spent, so let God use it to draw you closer to Him. At your next meeting, share with your group any key points or insights that stood out to you as you spent this time with the Lord.

PART ONE:
The Goal Is Unity

It is impossible to take in the sum of Scripture and *not* see God's "community priority." Beginning with the Trinity (where God the Father, God the Son, and God the Holy Spirit communed together as one), and culminating with the scene from Revelation (wherein every nation and every person gathers together in eternal unity), there is an emphasis on joining with other believers to gain strength, healing, and hope. But how are you to let others into your suffering, when your pain feels so distinctly *your own*? What will happen if you dismantle the protective fortress behind which you've been hiding? It is to these subjects we'll now turn.

REVISIT YOUR EXPERIENCE

Take a few moments to revisit this week's teaching as it relates to your personal experience.

Throughout the burdensome seasons you've walked through, have you typically trudged with others or alone? Was your choice made on purpose, or was it borne out of circumstances beyond your control?

What challenges have you known with regard to letting other people into your journey—the real stuff, the hard stuff, the pain?

What blessings have you experienced from "togetherness"? What is the upside to *not* walking alone?

RECEIVE GOD'S TRUTH

For this section, you'll need a Bible and quick fingers.

Look up the following verses, noting the "one-another" action that is encouraged, and then fill in the blanks.

- Mark 9:50: "Be at ____________ with each other."
- John 13:34: "____________ one another."
- Romans 12:10a: "Be ________ to one another in ________."
- Romans 12:10b: "Honor one another ________________________."
- Romans 12:16: "Live in ____________ with one another."
- Romans 15:7: "__________ one another, then, just as Christ ______________."
- 1 Corinthians 12:25: "Have _________________________ for each other."
- Galatians 5:13: "____________ one another humbly ____________."
- Ephesians 4:32: "Be ______ and _________________ to one another."
- Ephesians 5:19: "________ to one another with psalms, hymns, and songs . . ."
- Philippians 2:3: "In humility __________ others above yourselves."
- Colossians 3:16: "_________ and _________ one another with all ________."
- 1 Thessalonians 4:18: "Therefore ____________ one other."
- 1 Peter 5:5: "Clothe yourselves with _________________ toward one another."
- 1 John 4:11: "Since God so __________ us, we also ought to ________ one another."

These verses are but a portion of the fifty-nine "one-anothers" in Scripture. Why do you suppose these themes of community and unity are so close to the heart of God?

Given the verses you looked up, what benefits are to be gained by doing life together? Which of those benefits do you wish you could have in abundance today, and why?

As it relates to our subject of confessing brokenness to one another, look up these two final verses in your Bible, noting the command you find in each:

- Galatians 6:2: "__________ each other's ____________."
- James 5:16: "____________ your _________ to each other."

Compared with the other "one-anothers"—loving one another, being at peace with one another, welcoming one another—how easy or difficult do you find it to "bear each other's burdens" and "confess your sins to each other"?

Why do you think God places such a high value on our walking with each other not just when life is smooth sailing but also during turbulence and trial?

> Whoever conceals their sins does not prosper, but the one who confesses and renounces them finds mercy.
>
> (Proverbs 28:13)

What is the specific risk and the specific reward inherent in confessing your sins to one another?

What might "concealing" one's transgressions involve?

What connection does this verse imply between confessing your sins and forsaking them?

Describe in your own terms the "mercy" referred to here, which comes as a result of confessing to another person.

Why is obtaining mercy from another human being vital to the Christ-following life?

What fulfillment might you miss out on if you never know the mercy of another person in your life?

> About eight days after Jesus said this, he took Peter, John and James with him and went up onto a mountain to pray. As he was praying, the appearance of his face changed, and his clothes became as bright as a flash of lightning. Two men, Moses and Elijah, appeared in glorious splendor, talking with Jesus. They spoke about his departure, which he was about to bring to fulfillment at Jerusalem. Peter and his companions were very sleepy, but when they became fully awake, they saw his glory and the two men standing with him. As the men were leaving Jesus, Peter said to him, "Master, it is good for us to be here. Let us put up three shelters—one for you, one for Moses and one for Elijah." (He did not know what he was saying.)
>
> While he was speaking, a cloud appeared and covered them, and they were afraid as they entered the cloud. A voice came from the cloud, saying, "This is my Son, whom I have chosen; listen to him." When the voice had spoken, they found that Jesus was alone. The disciples kept this to themselves and did not tell anyone at that time what they had seen.
>
> (Luke 9:28–36)

Why did Jesus take Peter, John, and James with Him to the Mount of Transfiguration?

Why do you think Peter wanted to "put up three shelters" while there?

What emotions do you think Jesus and His disciples experienced there on the mount?

> Then Jesus went with his disciples to a place called Gethsemane, and he said to them, "Sit here while I go over there and pray." He took Peter and the two sons of Zebedee along with him, and he began to be sorrowful and troubled. Then he said to them, "My soul is overwhelmed with sorrow to the point of death. Stay here and keep watch with me."
>
> Going a little farther, he fell with his face to the ground and prayed, "My Father, if it is possible, may this cup be taken from me. Yet not as I will, but as you will."
>
> Then he returned to his disciples and found them sleeping. "Couldn't you men keep watch with me for one hour?" he asked Peter. "Watch and pray so that you will not fall into temptation. The spirit is willing, but the flesh is weak."
>
> He went away a second time and prayed, "My Father, if it is not possible for this cup to be taken away unless I drink it, may your will be done."
>
> When he came back, he again found them sleeping, because their eyes were heavy. So he left them and went away once more and prayed the third time, saying the same thing.
>
> Then he returned to the disciples and said to them, "Are you still sleeping and resting? Look, the hour has come, and the Son of Man is delivered into the hands of sinners. Rise! Let us go! Here comes my betrayer!"
>
> (Matthew 26:36–46)

Why do you think Jesus included His disciples in His moments of deepest agony and pain? Would you have made the same choice? Why or why not?

Do you think it was easier for Jesus to invite others into one of His "highest highs," there on the Mount of Transfiguration, or into His "lowest low" in the Garden of Gethsemane? Why?

What risks did Jesus face in allowing His disciples to know just how tormented He was by His imminent death on a Roman cross?

Do you think that Jesus's sharing His struggle led to His "obtaining mercy" from others there in the garden? Why or why not?

How might this "mercy" spoken of in Proverbs 28:13 come to us in a manner other than that which we expect?

Jesus saw fit to model something important for you and me in the way that he approached the cross. He didn't isolate. He didn't insulate. He didn't deny what was really real. Instead, he leaned into the strength and sureness of his community, and together, they suffered great pain. Together, they walked that impossible road. Together, they endured gut-wrenching grief.

—SHEILA WALSH

REORIENT YOUR HABITS AND HEART

As a means for bringing this theme to life—that of community being the means to achieving unity—select one or more of the following to practice sometime today:

- Memorize the "one another" passages of Scripture that you find the most challenging to practice faithfully.
- Watch a movie or read a book about someone with a powerful personal testimony, such as Elisabeth Elliot (*Through Gates of Splendor*), Billy Graham (*Just as I Am*), or Eric Liddell (*Chariots of Fire*). Think about the challenges they faced and how their stories have inspired people and brought unity.
- Journal a few of your own spiritual victories from the past. "Confess" challenges that God was faithful to help you overcome and practice telling one of those stories this week. It's less intimidating to share a challenge you've already faced, so start small in anticipation of progressing to present-day pain.
- Think of a time when a friend was "there for you" and write him or her a quick note. Thank your friend for having been a safe place for you during that time. Rehearse the benefits of interdependence as you send the note.

- Call or write to someone you know has been struggling and say, “I was thinking about you and wanted to offer a safe place for you should you ever want to talk.” Practice listening well to another’s confession as you work toward learning to confess the struggles you yourself face.

The confession of evil works is the first beginning of good works.

—SAINT AUGUSTINE

PART TWO: The Challenge Is Vulnerability

If there is one thing that keeps us from inviting others into the middle of our mess, it is our fear of being seen as weak or “not okay.” The mere mention of the word *vulnerability* can send shivers down our spines, and yet there is just no way to know the benefits of spiritual confession apart from laying ourselves open in the presence of others. The upside to this terrifying proposition is hearing the words “me too” from another person. And there is perhaps no more gratifying sound in the world than *words of empathy* to soothe our pain.

REVISIT YOUR EXPERIENCE

Think of a recent time when you practiced vulnerability in the presence of a trusted friend. Maybe you confided that your marriage has been challenging lately. Or maybe you admitted you’ve fallen into old, addictive patterns again. Or perhaps you owned up to the fact that you felt left out by a friend’s social-media post and had not been invited to a gathering she hosted.

Whatever the circumstances surrounding it, what led up to your moment of vulnerability?

What emotions did you experience as you shared what was on your mind?

What resulted from your telling your truth?

What did you learn about yourself as a result of the encounter?

What did you learn about God?

RECEIVE GOD'S TRUTH

Read the following Scripture passages and reflect on the related questions.

> One of those days Jesus went out to a mountainside to pray, and spent the night praying to God. When morning came, he called his disciples to him and chose twelve of them, whom he also designated apostles.
>
> (Luke 6:12–13)

Before Jesus called His twelve disciples to join Him in ministry and in life, He engaged in conversation with His Father through prayer. What is the significance of this?

How diligent are you to engage in conversation with God before practicing vulnerability and human confession?

What pain or awkwardness do you suspect would be avoided if you were always diligent in honoring this approach?

> Six days before the Passover, Jesus came to Bethany, where Lazarus lived, whom Jesus had raised from the dead. Here a dinner was given in Jesus' honor. Martha served, while Lazarus was among those reclining at the table with him. Then Mary took about a pint of pure nard, an expensive perfume; she poured it on Jesus' feet and wiped his feet with her hair. And the house was filled with the fragrance of the perfume.

> But one of his disciples, Judas Iscariot, who was later to betray him, objected, "Why wasn't this perfume sold and the money given to the poor? It was worth a year's wages." He did not say this because he cared about the poor but because he was a thief; as keeper of the money bag, he used to help himself to what was put into it.
>
> "Leave her alone," Jesus replied. "It was intended that she should save this perfume for the day of my burial. You will always have the poor among you, but you will not always have me."
>
> (John 12:1–8)

In this, one of the most powerful examples of vulnerability in Scripture, we find Mary anointing the feet of Jesus with expensive perfume. How might this image serve as a metaphor for divinely appointed, God-directed vulnerability in your life?

What is the connection between Mary's actions before Jesus and our wise but willing agreement to "pour ourselves out" in confession to another person?

How does vulnerability among Christ followers bless the heart of God?

Do you wish to rise? Begin by descending.
You plan a tower that will pierce the clouds?
Lay first the foundation of humility.

—SAINT AUGUSTINE

REORIENT YOUR HABITS AND HEART

To help activate the theme of risking vulnerability in sharing our struggles and pain, select one or more of the following endeavors to practice sometime today:

- Read the John 12 account of Mary anointing Jesus's feet to a loved one whom you deeply trust. Ask if the person would be willing for you to wash his or her feet as a sacrifice of praise to God. As you wash the person's feet, consider how humbling it feels to be exposed to this type of vulnerable service. If the person is willing, switch places. Does it feel more or less vulnerable to you to have your own feet washed?
- Write out the words to Proverbs 28:13, which says, "Whoever conceals their sins does not prosper, but the one who confesses and renounces them finds mercy." Ask God to reveal the specific "mercy" He has in store for you as you work toward confessing your sins to another person.
- Practice appropriate vulnerability by first praying to God for guidance. Bring to His attention a specific mess you've been in. Ask Him for insight about whom to trust with the truth of your situation, and then act on the divine direction you receive.
- The next time a friend or family member provides assistance to you, say, "Thank you for helping me," instead of just a quick, "Thanks." Practice receiving help. Practice acknowledging the help you've received. Practice experiencing what it feels like to be in the vulnerable position of needing help in the first place.

PART THREE:
The Benefit Is Hope on the Rise

As Sheila noted in this week's video segment, while the risks of vulnerability might feel sky-high, the rewards are higher still. God's mission has always been a communal one. As we engage in walking together through this life instead of going it alone, we will experience the hope of restoration rising up and lifting us all on its wings.

REVISIT YOUR EXPERIENCE

Think of a time when you relished the joy of togetherness, either with your family or with a group of friends. How was hope fostered in your spirit as you took in that scene?

In the video segment, Sheila related how her friend Sandi Patty offered her a precious gift when they went on a cruise together. During the trip, Sandi said, "Sheila, my cabin is our safe place on this ship. When you want to run away, run here. When you want to cry, cry here." In what ways have you witnessed this type of compassionate companionship in your life?

What character qualities are needed to offer such a gift to a friend?

If you could design your own "safe place"—a spot like Sandi's cabin room where you knew you were welcomed and would not be judged—what realities would be present there?

In my "safe place," these things would be true . . .

What is the connection between the realities you noted in the list and the concept of *hope on the rise*? How does your ability to tell your truth in a safe place foster hopefulness in your heart?

The friend who can be silent with us in a moment of despair or confusion, who can stay with us in an hour of grief and bereavement, who can tolerate not knowing . . . not healing, not curing . . . that is a friend who cares.

—HENRI NOUWEN

RECEIVE GOD'S TRUTH

Read the following Scripture passage and reflect on the related questions.

> Let us hold fast the confession of our hope without wavering, for he who promised is faithful. And let us consider how to stir up one another to love and good works, not neglecting to meet together, as is the habit of some, but encouraging one another, and all the more as you see the Day drawing near.
>
> (Hebrews 10:23–25 ESV)

What is the "confession of our hope" for those who are in Christ?

How does vulnerability in our relationships with others "stir" us up toward love and good works?

When have you experienced such a "stirring up"? What circumstances were at work, and what usefulness did vulnerability and confession provide?

How might confession—revealing your truth to another person for the purpose of finding healing for your soul—rekindle hope for you?

Why does it require depth of connection with another human being in order to make deeply spiritual gains, such as restoring hope in your mind and heart?

What does this connection between depth of relationship and spiritual growth reveal about how effectively you are growing today?

REORIENT YOUR HABITS AND HEART

To confirm this theme of hope rising as a result of your willingness to engage in honest confession with others, consider the question, "Will you be known by those who come behind you as one who let others in?" Your life will leave behind the fragrance of hope on the rise as a result of the unity and community you sought out, or it will leave behind the scent of solitude . . . of isolation at its worst. As Sheila writes in *In the Middle of the Mess*:

> I had wanted to be able to share Mum's darkest moments and know what she felt. I didn't want her to cry alone, but looking at the photo of Maureen, I began to see that she really hadn't been alone. She'd allowed her closest friends into that sacred space where her truest self lived. Mum had her community, a safe group of sisters to whom she could confess those things most people hide from even God. They were her sisters of confession and prayer, and they made a place where grief and joy, hopes and dreams, darkness and light could be shared.
>
> As a child I'd built a walled-off hiding place that was intended to protect myself from being hurt by others. I thought she had too. Looking back now, though, I don't think that was true. Mum knew she needed more than confession to her heavenly Father. She needed a safe community where she could be vulnerable, a community that would love her amid her vulnerability. She found it in her

community of sisters. And through walking with those sisters, I think Mum discovered the secret to the depth of salvation, to bringing her most authentic self to Christ. She wasn't a woman marked by her pain. She was intimately known and accepted. She was well-loved.

In the space provided on page 129, write out a prayer to God in which you declare the type of person you hope to become and the type of legacy you want to leave.

Few things accelerate the peace process as much as humbly admitting our own wrongdoing and asking forgiveness.

—LEE STROBEL

PRACTICING THE DISCIPLINE OF TELLING THE TRUTH

The act of confessing your struggle to another person is something like a muscle. When you neglect it, it tends to atrophy; but when you flex it, it becomes strong. You may have "stuffed" the pain of your struggle for so long that even when reading about confession, you find yourself woefully post-workout sore. But take heart: a few reps today, a few more reps tomorrow, and soon you'll be racing the wind. If you're ready to get better at telling the truth to your loved ones, the following two steps are for you. Give them a try, and see how you feel as you go. Are you getting stronger, day by day?

1. Start with God, but Don't Stay There

As previously stated, all proper confession should begin with a time of prayer, during which you bring your struggles before the Lord and seek His insight as to whom to tell. But at some point, it's time to act on that direction. It's time to go find the person you've been directed to tell *and speak out those words you must say.*

2. Start Small, but Don't Stay There

Once you are in the presence of the person to whom you plan to tell your truth, go ahead and admit any fears lurking inside your heart. Say, "This conversation I need to have with you feels *terrifying*. But I'm committed to talking, if you're committed to listening. Should we keep going?" Even that small act of vulnerability will pave the way for more to come. Go slowly through this experience, but indeed, *choose to go*.

That pain we fear might just do us in? Something about someone showing up to shoulder part of that load . . . it injects us with courage and hope.

—SHEILA WALSH

Before the next meeting, read chapters 9 and 10 of *In the Middle of the Mess.*

Session Five

Brokenness Is the Path to Healing

Gratitude in the Middle of the Mess

Gratitude bestows reverence, allowing us to encounter everyday epiphanies, those transcendent moments of awe that change forever how we experience life and the world.

John Milton

Session Overview

It's an odd progression. We struggle through suffering—grieving the sting, the sorrow, the hopelessness, the loss we feel—only to discover that there in our grieving, we encounter Jesus, the One who faithfully wipes away tears. We come to God in a spirit of humility, knowing that He alone can rescue us from the state we're in, and there, in our conversations with God, we are emboldened to let others know of our pain. So we go; we invite; we speak truth; we lay bare—sure that unity gets ushered in no other way. We do these things because no other thing has worked, and, astoundingly, as we do them, we emerge on the other side . . . whole.

Yes, our circumstances still taunt us.

Yes, our hearts still ache with the great not-yet.

Yes, our stance still gets shaky.

But we're here. We're standing. We're whole.

In truth, we're far more than that. We're *grateful* for the pain we've known.

How is this possible? It is possible because we have seen that these victories, small though they seem at the time, are but a foretaste of a far grander victory to come. A victory that is yours and mine to claim.

Opening Thoughts

Take one to two minutes to open your time together with prayer. Then, have each group member answer the following questions before watching the video segment:

What is a highlight from your between-sessions learning that you would like to share with the group?

As you look back on your life, what was a situation that was ridiculously tough to walk through at the time, but you're now grateful for today?

Video: Brokenness Is the Path to Healing (20 MINUTES)

Play the video for Session 5. Use the following prompts to record your thoughts as you watch.

VIDEO NOTES

When all the old tricks don't work

The temptation to rebuild the unhelpful walls you've torn down

Things are as they should be

Where your need leads

On “presenting ourselves”

The thorn in Paul’s flesh

The power that’s perfected in weakness

Set-apartness

To power up, or to suit up

The newness that brokenness yields

The battle is *God's*, not ours

Group Discussion

Spend the balance of your group time answering as many of the following questions as you have time and energy for, being sure to give equal opportunity for each member to share.

1. What is a phrase or concept from this session's video segment that you found especially useful or meaningful? Why was it so impactful for you?

2. Sheila mentioned what is perhaps the biggest revelation she has received regarding brokenness: "My distinct need, when handled maturely, leads me to God's distinct ability to meet it." How did this comment strike you? In what ways does your experience square with this idea?

3. When have you known the blessings or fruitfulness of having "presented yourself" or "handed yourself over" to Christ from the midst of your pain? What were the circumstances? What occurred as a result?

4. If God is able to glorify himself through your pain, as Sheila mentioned, does this mean He "stirs up" challenging situations for you just to receive the glory they may provide? Why or why not?

5. When confronted with brokenness, suffering, and strife, we tend to ask one of two questions: "Why is God allowing this to happen?" or, "Will I choose to worship God in light of His choice?" Which question tends to represent your attitude in your present circumstances? What factors fuel that choice?

6. What character qualities do you think need to be present in a person who faithfully "suits up" with the armor of God?

Closing Prayer

Taking as much time as your group needs, have each member who feels comfortable complete the following prayer prompt as a way to close your discussion:

God, if I were to express gratitude for one aspect of this suffering I've been going through, I would tell you that . . .

Between-Sessions Personal Study

Session Five

Reflect on the content you've discussed this week by engaging in any or all of the following between-sessions personal studies. The time you invest will be well spent, so let God use it to draw you closer to Him. At your next meeting, share with your group any key points or insights that stood out to you as you spent this time with the Lord.

PART ONE:
The Battle Points Us to God

This battle we've been in the midst of? It never was intended to do us in. No, such a scenario would put the focus on us. This battle is part of a larger *war*, in which God sits, center stage. This battle we've known, like every battle that's *ever* been known, is being fought for the glory of God. When we are weak, He is strong. When we are suffering, He will prevail. When we are knocked down, He rises up. When we fall away, He stands firm.

REVISIT YOUR EXPERIENCE

In this session's video segment, Sheila reflected on her sixtieth birthday. Here is what she said:

Around the same time as that dreadful, rain-soaked trip to the Gulf of Mexico, my body had the audacity to turn sixty years old. Sixty! I could hardly believe it.

My husband and son had done everything they could think to do to distract me from the sadness over Mum's death, gifting me with a pink leather jacket and a hand-painted trophy, respectively. But even amid such lovely gifts, my heart sank low in my chest.

It was my first birthday without Mum. There would be no birthday call. There would be no birthday song. Mum couldn't really sing in tune, but I loved it anyway. There would be no celebration. There would be little more than grief.

By then, I knew what signs to watch for—signs that the problem inside of me was gaining ground. This is the peril of clinical depression. It can rear its ugly head again, just when we think it's under control.

My mind chased to solutions I'd relied on through the years: prayer, the Word of God, exercise, meds. *Why weren't they helping me now?*

I couldn't concentrate. I couldn't sleep. I couldn't make myself engage with my friends, even as I knew that I should.

Do you want to know what I felt like doing—the only thing that sounded appealing to me? I wanted to get out my fortress blueprints and start erecting the thing all over again. I was spiraling downward faster and faster, wondering where I'd finally land. And who I'd be, once I did.

What are some triggers in your life that make you want to get out your "fortress blueprints" and set up walls?

Have you ever made real progress in working through a particular struggle, only to backtrack in a meaningful way? What were the circumstances involved?

How did the experience impact your mind and heart?

In what ways did the reemergence of the pain serve to draw you *back* to God?

Pain removes the veil; it plants the flag of truth within the fortress of a rebel soul.

—C. S. LEWIS

RECEIVE GOD'S TRUTH

Read the following Scripture passages and reflect on the related questions.

> He said to me, "My grace is sufficient for you, for my power is made perfect in weakness." Therefore I will boast all the more gladly about my weaknesses, so

> that Christ's power may rest on me. That is why, for Christ's sake, I delight in weaknesses, in insults, in hardships, in persecutions, in difficulties. For when I am weak, then I am strong.
>
> (2 Corinthians 12:9–10)

Paul had been given "a thorn" in his flesh, "a messenger of Satan" to torment him (see verses 7–8). But when he asked for the Lord to take it away, he received this response. What does it mean that God makes His power perfect in the midst of our weakness?

What shift occurred in Paul's mind and heart upon realizing that God was not, in fact, going to remove the thorn?

What words of consolation did God offer to Paul regarding how to think about this thorn that was not going to be removed?

> Therefore, since we are surrounded by such a great cloud of witnesses, let us throw off everything that hinders and the sin that so easily entangles. And let us run with perseverance the race marked out for us, fixing our eyes on Jesus, the pioneer and perfecter of faith. For the joy set before him he endured the cross, scorning its shame, and sat down at the right hand of the throne of God.
>
> (Hebrews 12:1–2)

What motivated Jesus to endure the suffering of the cross with such grace?

What "joy" was set before Jesus? How is this same joy available to Christ followers today?

Any discussion of how pain and suffering fit into God's scheme ultimately leads back to the cross.

—PHILIP YANCEY

What character qualities were on display as Jesus endured the suffering that God allowed in His life? Check all that apply.

- ☐ Understanding
- ☐ Compassion
- ☐ Joy
- ☐ Perspective
- ☐ Love
- ☐ Patience
- ☐ Others-centeredness
- ☐ Longsuffering
- ☐ Optimism
- ☐ Contentment
- ☐ Peacefulness
- ☐ Righteousness

Which quality might you know in greater abundance if you shifted your focus more regularly from your immediate struggle to God's eternal glory?

This is what the LORD says—
    he who made a way through the sea,
    a path through the mighty waters,
who drew out the chariots and horses,
    the army and reinforcements together,
and they lay there, never to rise again,
    extinguished, snuffed out like a wick:
"Forget the former things;
    do not dwell on the past.
See, I am doing a new thing!
    Now it springs up; do you not perceive it?
I am making a way in the wilderness
    and streams in the wasteland.
The wild animals honor me,
    the jackals and the owls,
because I provide water in the wilderness
    and streams in the wasteland,
to give drink to my people, my chosen,
    the people I formed for myself
    that they may proclaim my praise."

(ISAIAH 43:16–21)

What images does this passage provide as alternatives to our fixating on our mess?

Which of the images brings you the most joy to consider? Why?

What encouragement can you gain from knowing God is aware of your struggle here in the "mighty waters," your wrestling here in the "wasteland," your desperation here in the "desert"? What comfort does His awareness bring whenever a "backtrack" day shows up?

Deny your weakness, and you will never know God's strength in you.

—JONI EARECKSON TADA

REORIENT YOUR HABITS AND HEART

As a means for bringing to life this theme—the battles that we face serving to point us back to God—select one or more of the following to practice sometime today:

- Take a nature walk. View the water, the land, and the animals you see as conduits of God's coming glory. How can these simple, everyday emblems transport you from the middle of your mess to a place of perspective and peace?
- Write God a letter of apology for a time when you sought your own glory more than His.
- Memorize a phrase from Isaiah 43 and carry it with you this week. Or read Isaiah 43:16–21 aloud each morning this week as a means of resetting your focus on Him.
- Speak of God's goodness and grandeur this week. Say His name. Declare His fame. Honor Him in the conversations you have.
- Acknowledge someone who glorifies God in his or her life and speech. Tell that person what a blessing he or she is in your life.

PART TWO:
The Battle Is Fought by God

As Sheila noted in the teaching, the events surrounding her birthday led to a striking revelation: "My distinct need, when handled maturely, leads me to God's distinct ability to meet it." Our need points us to God, who alone can meet those needs. It is He who fights the battles we face! As the prophet Ezra reminded God's people, "Do not be afraid or discouraged because of this vast army. For the battle is not yours, but God's" (2 Chronicles 20:15). We need to lift our gaze from our struggle to our Savior, for it is *He* who has waged this war in which we find ourselves. This battle is fought by Him.

REVISIT YOUR EXPERIENCE

What is your reaction to the idea that the battle you've been fighting is actually God's, not yours, to fight?

How effectively have your "battle strategies" been for you? In what ways might the Lord prove to be a better strategist than you?

What fears or concerns stand in the way of your conceding this battle fully to the Lord?

RECEIVE GOD'S TRUTH

Read the following Scripture passages and reflect on the related questions.

> Therefore, I urge you, brothers and sisters, in view of God's mercy, to offer your bodies as a living sacrifice, holy and pleasing to God—this is your true and proper worship. Do not conform to the pattern of this world, but be transformed by the renewing of your mind. Then you will be able to test and approve what God's will is—his good, pleasing and perfect will.
>
> (Romans 12:1–2)

In this session's video segment, Sheila explained that to "present" yourself means to *offer*, once and for all. What do you suppose this one-time commitment involves as it relates to dealing with pain?

What does Paul suggest is the conduit that allows this sacrificial offering to occur?

In what ways might the world threaten your commitment to present yourself sacrificially to God?

What does a "renewed mind" have to do with your ability to faithfully present yourself to God?

> Finally, be strong in the Lord and in his mighty power. Put on the full armor of God, so that you can take your stand against the devil's schemes. For our struggle is not against flesh and blood, but against the rulers, against the authorities, against the powers of this dark world and against the spiritual forces of evil in the heavenly realms. Therefore put on the full armor of God, so that when the day of evil comes, you may be able to stand your ground, and after you have done everything, to stand. Stand firm then, with the belt of truth buckled around your waist, with the breastplate of righteousness in place, and with your feet fitted with the readiness that comes from the gospel of peace. In addition to all this, take up the shield of faith, with which you can extinguish all the flaming arrows of the evil one. Take the helmet of salvation and the sword of the Spirit, which is the word of God. And pray in the Spirit on all occasions with all kinds of prayers and requests. With this in mind, be alert and always keep on praying for all the Lord's people.
>
> (Ephesians 6:10–18)

In the video segment, Sheila noted the difference between "powering up" and "suiting up." How would these "weapons" and forms of battle gear differ, if the battle were yours, not the Lord's?

How does each of the aspects of God's armor help you gain perspective and strength in your battle? Note your thoughts below.

Verse	Piece of Armor	How This Gives Strength for Your Battle
6:14	Belt of truth	
6:14	Breastplate of righteousness	
6:15	[Shoes of] the gospel of peace	
6:16	Shield of faith	
6:17	Helmet of salvation	
6:17	Sword of the Spirit	

What practice could you implement to more faithfully and intentionally "put on" the whole armor of God?

> Do you not know?
> Have you not heard?
> The Lord is the everlasting God,
> the Creator of the ends of the earth.
> He will not grow tired or weary,
> and his understanding no one can fathom.
> He gives strength to the weary
> and increases the power of the weak.

Even youths grow tired and weary,
 and young men stumble and fall;
but those who hope in the LORD
 will renew their strength.
They will soar on wings like eagles;
 they will run and not grow weary,
 they will walk and not be faint.

(ISAIAH 40:28–31)

What assumptions does the prophet Isaiah make about the struggles we will encounter throughout this earthly existence?

What promise do you find in this passage regarding your ability to thrive even in the midst of great pain?

What connection do you see between a Christ follower's faithfulness in "suiting up" with the armor of God and his or her enjoyment of God-given energy, stability, and strength?

REORIENT YOUR HABITS AND HEART

To help reinforce this theme of how the Lord is fighting the battle for you, select one or more of the following to practice sometime today:

- Curl your hands into fists and then release them, fingers relaxed, hands open, arms down. Remind yourself of the phrase, "My battle is the Lord's." What emotions come to the surface as you remind yourself to whom "your" battle belongs? Bring those findings to the Lord in prayer.
- Write out an acrostic for the word *FIGHT*, where each letter reflects God's role in this battle. For instance, the *F* might stand for "faithful guide." Beside the I you might write "inspiring commander." Do this for all five letters.
- As you get dressed in the morning, list off the various parts of the armor of God, asking God to help you spiritually "suit up" for the day ahead.

PART THREE:
The Battle Is Won by God

The thought of actually feeling grateful for your suffering might seem ludicrous to you at first. But remember that not only does God fight your battles, He always *wins* them for you. With this in mind, you see how practical and rational it is to be *grateful for the mess*.

REVISIT YOUR EXPERIENCE

Describe a time you've engaged in some activity—watching a sporting event, re-reading a book, screening a movie you know by heart—even when you knew what the outcome would be. What is the emotional experience of being assured things will work out a certain way?

What encouragement do you take from the idea that, in spite of the challenges and struggles you face in this life, God assures His followers victory in the end?

RECEIVE GOD'S TRUTH

Read the following Scripture passages and reflect on the related questions.

> Then I saw "a new heaven and a new earth," for the first heaven and the first earth had passed away, and there was no longer any sea. I saw the Holy City, the new Jerusalem, coming down out of heaven from God, prepared as a bride beautifully dressed for her husband. And I heard a loud voice from the throne saying, "Look! God's dwelling place is now among the people, and he will dwell with them. They will be his people, and God himself will be with them and be their God. 'He will wipe every tear from their eyes. There will be no more death' or mourning or crying or pain, for the old order of things has passed away."
>
> He who was seated on the throne said, "I am making everything new!" Then he said, "Write this down, for these words are trustworthy and true."
>
> He said to me: "It is done. I am the Alpha and the Omega, the Beginning and the End. To the thirsty I will give water without cost from the spring of the water of life. Those who are victorious will inherit all this, and I will be their God and they will be my children."
>
> (Revelation 21:1–7)

Which aspect of the current reality will you be most excited to leave behind? Why?

Which aspect of the coming reality appeals most to you? Why?

How does this image of a new heaven and a new earth, where there will be no mourning, no crying, and no death, inspire you to persist despite present pain?

What phrases would you use to describe how you hope to look back on this present suffering you've been made to endure from that place in the reality to come?

Faith is the strength by which a shattered world shall emerge into the light.

—HELEN KELLER

REORIENT YOUR HABITS AND HEART

In her book *In the Middle of the Mess*, Sheila writes:

> There's a powerful visual of what that looks like in the film adaptation of the fourth book in The Chronicles of Narnia, *Prince Caspian*. It's not 100 percent true to the book, but it's quite lovely anyway. In the film, Lucy says to Aslan, "I wish I was braver." Aslan replies, "If you were any braver, you would be a lioness."

So Lucy walks alone onto the bridge and faces the vast Telmarine Army. The army stops for a moment, stunned to see a young girl blocking their way. It's a David and Goliath moment.

With a small smile, Lucy draws out her dagger and waves it at them. That's when Aslan begins to pace with deliberate steps just behind her, and we know why she's not afraid.

She's not alone.

Neither are we.

To help confirm this theme that God has assured you of victory at the end of this fight, spend a few moments picturing yourself suited up for battle, with the Lion of Judah proudly pacing before you, behind you, and around you.

Don't you see it? We've already arrived, there at the place we've been searching for. In his presence, there is comfort. In his power, there is peace. In his provision, there is abundance. In his protection, we're always safe.

—SHEILA WALSH

PRACTICING THE DISCIPLINE OF GRATITUDE

It is true: you can feel grateful from here in the mess, because you know that God is on the move—in you, around you, through you, for you. Because of His activity, you've already arrived at the place of victory over the struggle you were sure would take you down. The irony is this: for all of the losses you've experienced, *truly, you've already won.*

1. Look Up from the Mess

Are you eager for your suffering to be beautifully and miraculously reframed? Start by looking up from the mess you've been in the middle of, to see your Father, there at your side.

2. Lean into God

Next, lean into your Father's presence, remembering this battle isn't yours to fight. As Paul wrote, "If God is for us, who can be against us? He who did not spare his own Son, but gave him up for us all—how will he not also, along with him, graciously give us all things? . . . In all these things we are more than conquerors through him who loved us" (Romans 8:31–32, 37).

3. Be Thankful

Finally, thank God for allowing this challenge in your life, which has brought you into deeper intimacy with Him. Thank Him for perfecting His power in your weakness and for providing grace that really is sufficient for you. In the space provided on the next page, write out your prayer today to God.

Before the next meeting, read chapters 11 and 12 of *In the Middle of the Mess.*

Session Six

Brokenness Is Temporary

Worshiping Christ Our Light

The Lord is my light and my salvation; whom shall I fear?
The Lord is the stronghold of my life; of whom shall I be afraid?

Psalm 27:1 ESV

Session Overview

When you're in the midst of dark times, it's easy to believe you'll never know light again. In the thick of a raging thunderstorm, it can seem as if the blanket of clouds will never disburse. Surrounded by the cloak of midnight, you have trouble believing a new day will ever break. And in your bleakest times emotionally, you are *sure* that the sun won't rise.

However, just because you find a place familiar—as Sheila will remind us in this session—it doesn't mean that place is where you *belong*. In this sixth and final installment, we will look at the legacy left by those who choose to live light. Not only do they unburden themselves before God, which in turn lightens their *emotional* load, but they also choose spreading the grace and peace—spiritual "light"—to those stuck in the grip of darkness.

Opening Thoughts

Take one to two minutes to open your time together with prayer. Then, have each group member answer the following questions before watching the video segment:

What is a highlight from your between-sessions learning that you would like to share with the group?

When have you experienced total physical darkness? What circumstances were involved? What emotions bubbled up in you as you realized that you *just couldn't see*?

Video: Brokenness Is Temporary (20.5 MINUTES)

Play the video for Session 6. Use the following prompts to record your thoughts as you watch.

VIDEO NOTES

Blazing sunshine lighting up the darkness all around

Leaving the light of Christ as our legacy

Secret struggles are more believable in the dark

Bodies dying, even as spirits are being renewed

Preparing for the weight of God's glory

Psalm 23: the burden is not ours, but His

On yielding our flickering torch to the one, true Light of the world

The Lord as light, salvation, and stronghold

In our darkness is rising powerful light

Which one does Jesus love?

Group Discussion

Spend the balance of your group time answering as many of the following questions as you have time and energy for, being sure to give equal opportunity for each member to share.

1. Which aspect of this session's video segment did you find most compelling, and why?

2. How would seeing your present place of brokenness as a temporary stop help you to reframe the situation and hang onto hope?

3. What challenges would you foresee in choosing to view your weighty load, your heavy burden, your besetting struggles, as "light and momentary troubles," as the apostle Paul calls them in 2 Corinthians 4:17?

4. What encouragement do the words of Psalm 23 offer to you as you work to take in a longer view of your present trials and tribulation?

5. In what ways have you found it difficult to assume a "posture of belovedness," as Sheila describes it, from there in the middle of your mess?

6. How might your legacy to your friends and family look different if you were to fully receive the light and love of God?

Closing Prayer

Taking as much time as your group needs, have each member who feels comfortable complete the following prayer prompt as a way to close your discussion:

God, as I consider pursuing this life of light and love with greater fervency, would you please deepen in me the desire for . . .

Final Personal Study

Session Six

Reflect on the content you've discussed this week by engaging in any or all of the following personal studies. The time you invest will be well spent, so let God use it to draw you closer to Him. Sometime in the coming days, share with a group member, friend, or family member any key points or insights that stood out to you as you spent this time with the Lord.

PART ONE:
"Living Light" Means Choosing Life

"Living light" is first a choice for *life*. It is standing against death in all its forms—spiritual, emotional, physical, financial, relational, behavioral, and more—and choosing life instead.

REVISIT YOUR EXPERIENCE

Take a few moments to revisit this week's teaching as it relates to your personal experience.

Describe a time when you were faced with a certain death of some kind—in a friendship, in your marriage, in a positive habit—but were able to choose life instead. How did that choice affect other positive choices you made?

In her book *In the Middle of the Mess*, Sheila talks about her perseverance even as she faced yet another round of temptations to end her life. She writes:

> As I've learned that God is my safe place, I've learned to confess all my secret pain, all my unspoken hurts. It doesn't mean there won't be pain; it just means I won't keep it hidden any longer. I'll bring it all into His presence—the sorrow, questions, anger, sadness. I bring the joy and laugher too. Every emotion, every feeling, every thought is welcomed. And so, in that bathroom, I turned to my safe place.
>
> I sat quietly for a while. I asked God to speak to the darkness. In the stillness I heard my Father speak to the deepest, safest place inside me.
>
> "I'm proud of you. I love you so much. I've never missed a moment of your life. I've been there all along, and I'm right here now."
>
> I hadn't known it, but this was what I'd been waiting for. This was what I wanted to hear and know. I raised my arms as if in worship, but it felt more like a daughter raising her arms to her dad so that he could pick her up. I felt like letting go—of the anger, sorrow, and pain. It felt like what I can only describe as joy—pure, undiluted joy.
>
> There, in that bathroom, I thought back on so many of the moments when I'd felt alone. I remember summer camp one year, when the dads were invited to spend the day with their kids. I hid in my room until it was over. I remembered walking along the beach when I was sixteen years old. Mum was in surgery and I knew it was serious, and I was afraid of being left alone. So many moments played before my eyes like an old black-and-white movie reel. I realized that I've always seen myself as a lonely girl. But there, I was learning the truth: Though I felt lonely and scared, I was the well-loved girl of God.

And though these feelings of loneliness were familiar, I was coming into an understanding: Just because a place has become familiar doesn't mean it's where you belong.

How would you describe the blessing of perseverance that Sheila realized in this story?

What divinely placed realization would she have missed out on if she had made a different choice?

What blessings of perseverance might be waiting for you on the other side of this present pain?

Imperfection is the prerequisite for grace.
Light only gets in through the cracks.

—PHILLIPS BROOKS

RECEIVE GOD'S TRUTH

Read the following Scripture passages and reflect on the related questions.

> But we have this treasure in jars of clay to show that this all-surpassing power is from God and not from us. We are hard pressed on every side, but not crushed; perplexed, but not in despair; persecuted, but not abandoned; struck down, but not destroyed. We always carry around in our body the death of Jesus, so that the life of Jesus may also be revealed in our body. For we who are alive are always being given over to death for Jesus' sake, so that his life may also be revealed in our mortal body. So then, death is at work in us, but life is at work in you.
>
> (2 Corinthians 4:7–12)

Put words to the resilience you see manifested in this passage—especially as it pertains to *choosing life*.

How would you describe the difference between the contrasts set up in this passage—affliction versus being crushed; persecution versus being forsaken, and so forth?

What kind of "death" is encouraged in this passage, and for what purpose?

What is your personal experience with this sort of death?

> Therefore we do not lose heart. Though outwardly we are wasting away, yet inwardly we are being renewed day by day. For our light and momentary troubles are achieving for us an eternal glory that far outweighs them all. So we fix our eyes not on what is seen, but on what is unseen, since what is seen is temporary, but what is unseen is eternal.
>
> (2 Corinthians 4:16–18)

What reason does Paul cite for why we don't lose heart, even in the midst of tribulation and trials?

What does "inner" renewal encompass? What sort of inner renewal have you known along the way?

In what ways does bearing the burden of brokenness prepare us for an eternity spent seeking God's glory?

What other observations can you make regarding perseverance through affliction and the renewal that is to come from the verses that follow? Note your findings on the grid.

Scripture Reference	Observations
Be joyful in hope, patient in affliction, faithful in prayer (Romans 12:12).	
Being strengthened with all power according to his glorious might so that you may have great endurance and patience, and giving joyful thanks to the Father, who has qualified you to share in the inheritance of his holy people in the kingdom of light (Colossians 1:11–12).	
Let us not become weary in doing good, for at the proper time we will reap a harvest if we do not give up (Galatians 6:9).	
Praise be to the God and Father of our Lord Jesus Christ, the Father of compassion and the God of all comfort, who comforts us in all our troubles, so that we can comfort those in any trouble with the comfort we ourselves receive from God (2 Corinthians 1:3–4).	

What encouragement can you draw from these verses as you choose life over death today?

> *"The thief comes only to steal and kill and destroy; I have come that they may have life, and have it to the full."*
>
> —JESUS (JOHN 10:10)

REORIENT YOUR HABITS AND HEART

As a means for putting into action this theme—that of choosing life as the first step in "living light"—select one or more of the following to practice sometime today:

- Sit in a perfectly dark room, and then flip on the light. How does your awareness of the things around you shift? Write a prayer to God, asking Him to give you greater perspective regarding the pain you've been walking through.
- Create a manifesto regarding your choice for life. List the various forms of "death" that threaten to overtake you, and then create statements of life to stand against each one.
- Using Paul's words from 2 Corinthians 4:7–18, imagine the things that have tried to press you, perplex you, knock you over, or hunt you down. Now picture a huge beam of light surrounding you, creating an impenetrable field that pushes the darkness away. What does physical light do to physical darkness? How does the light of the Lord push spiritual darkness away? Meditate on this thought.

PART TWO:
"Living Light" Means Pursuing Peace

In addition to standing against every form of darkness as a means for "living light," we see along this journey that the person who craves the light of the Lord craves also *impenetrable peace*. If ever there were a worthwhile picture of such tranquility, Psalm 23 paints that view.

REVISIT YOUR EXPERIENCE

What does it look like for you to push past life's chaos and carve out a few moments of peace? Consider the harried mom who is determined to have five minutes of meaningful conversation with a beloved friend over a cup of tea. She invites her friend into the living room, offers her a seat on the couch, gently pushes an arm across the inches-thick blanket of Legos covering the coffee table, and, with a smile, says, "Please, set down your tea and relax."

Or think of the businessman who excuses himself from the boardroom at the strike of the hour, right when the chairman promised the meeting would be done. He makes his way across town to his son's soccer game—the championship game, no less.

Or what about the twentysomething woman wracked by addiction, who turns up on the church's front steps? She slips in, unannounced, and makes her way to a pew—to sit there in the silence and pray.

When Sheila asked at that conference for anyone who had walked the "lonely, terrifying path" of recurring suicidal thoughts and of cutting, every woman who rose from her seat and came forward was pursuing real peace.

What about you? When was the last time you pushed pause on the chaos surrounding you and *demanded* for peace to take its place?

What were the circumstances surrounding the experience? What did "peace" look like for you then?

RECEIVE GOD'S TRUTH

Read the following Scripture passages and reflect on the related questions.

> The LORD is my shepherd, I lack nothing.
> He makes me lie down in green pastures,
> he leads me beside quiet waters,
> he refreshes my soul.
> He guides me along the right paths
> for his name's sake.
> Even though I walk
> through the darkest valley,
> I will fear no evil,
> for you are with me;
> your rod and your staff,
> they comfort me.
>
> You prepare a table before me
> in the presence of my enemies.
> You anoint my head with oil;
> my cup overflows.
> Surely your goodness and love will follow me
> all the days of my life,
> and I will dwell in the house of the LORD
> forever.
>
> (PSALM 23:1–6)

For many people, the words of Psalm 23 bring to mind vivid memories of times past. When did you first encounter these verses? What meaning do they carry for you?

What emotions rise to the surface for you as you take in the imagery of this psalm?

Which parts of this psalm seem most "peaceful" to you, and why?

What comes to mind when you think of God as your "Shepherd"?

What are some of the aspects of life over which you see peace being declared in this passage? For example, the opening phrase, "the LORD is my Shepherd," declares peace over the *leadership of our lives*. The phrase, "I lack nothing," declares peace over *the desires of our heart*. Fill in the table for the rest of the phrases:

The Phrase . . .	**Declares Peace Over This Area of Life . . .**
The LORD is my Shepherd	The leadership of my life
I lack nothing	The desires of my heart
He makes me lie down in green pastures	
He leads me beside still waters	
He refreshes my soul	
He guides me along the right paths	

The Phrase . . .	**Declares Peace Over This Area of Life . . .**
I will fear no evil, for you are with me	
Your rod and staff, they comfort me	
You prepare a table before me in the presence of my enemies	
You anoint my head with oil	
My cup overflows	
Surely your goodness and love will follow me all the days of my life	
I will dwell in the house of the Lord forever	

"Though I have been speaking figuratively, a time is coming when I will no longer use this kind of language but will tell you plainly about my Father. In that day you will ask in my name. I am not saying that I will ask the Father on your behalf. No, the Father himself loves you because you have loved me and have believed that I came from God. I came from the Father and entered the world; now I am leaving the world and going back to the Father."

Then Jesus' disciples said, "Now you are speaking clearly and without figures of speech. Now we can see that you know all things and that you do not even need to have anyone ask you questions. This makes us believe that you came from God."

"Do you now believe?" Jesus replied. "A time is coming and in fact has come when you will be scattered, each to your own home. You will leave me all alone. Yet I am not alone, for my Father is with me.

"I have told you these things, so that in me you may have peace. In this world you will have trouble. But take heart! I have overcome the world."

(John 16:25–33)

What "hour" is Jesus referring to in this passage?

What does Jesus mean when He says to "take heart"?

In what way has Jesus "overcome the world"?

How can the disciples be expected to "take heart" and "have peace" when Jesus is leaving their presence for good?

What encouragement does this passage offer regarding how you can *take heart* and *have peace*?

REORIENT YOUR HABITS AND HEART

To help activate this theme of pursuing peace, select one or more of the following to practice sometime today:

- Listen to calming music as you write out the words of Psalm 23. Read them aloud once, twice, three times—slowly, steadily, meaningfully.
- Meditate on the declaration, "I am a person of peace. Peace toward myself. Peace toward others. Peace toward God."
- Look at your schedule for today and ask God what it might look like to "bring peace" to each of those engagements, meetings, conversations, and tasks.

PART THREE:
"Living Light" Means Living Loved

There is a third aspect to "living light," which is to receive the love God has for you, assuming the "posture of belovedness" that Sheila mentions in this session's video segment. In truth, you are no longer a slave to fear; you are a child of God.

REVISIT YOUR EXPERIENCE

Take a few moments to think about the way in which God sees you, as His beloved child.

When have you received even a glimpse of God's great love for you?

What were the circumstances involved in the experience? How did the realization impact you?

What do you stand to gain from seeing yourself as "beloved," even in the middle of a troubling mess?

RECEIVE GOD'S TRUTH

Read the following Scripture passages and reflect on the related questions.

> The LORD your God is with you,
> the Mighty Warrior who saves.
> He will take great delight in you;
> in his love he will no longer rebuke you,
> but will rejoice over you with singing.
>
> (ZEPHANIAH 3:17)

What expression do you envision on God's face as He rejoices over you "with gladness"?

Rewrite this verse as a love note from God to you. What would that note say?

> But you, Lord, are a compassionate and gracious God,
> slow to anger, abounding in love and faithfulness.
>
> (PSALM 86:15)

Why is it important that the God you serve is "slow to anger"?

What does it mean for God to be "abounding in love and faithfulness" for you?

> See what great love the Father has lavished on us, that we should be called children of God! And that is what we are! The reason the world does not know us is that it did not know him.
>
> (1 John 3:1)

What kind of love do you picture the Father having for you, if He so freely calls you His child?

What is "the world" missing out on if they don't know this love from God?

What do you hope to not miss out on regarding the lavish love of your heavenly Father? In what ways do you long to draw closer to Him?

The Lord is my light and my salvation—whom shall I fear? The Lord is the stronghold of my life—of whom shall I be afraid?

—DAVID (PSALM 27:1)

REORIENT YOUR HABITS AND HEART

In an effort to confirm God's love for her and her love for God each day, Sheila established a "who-I-am" place. As she explains in her book *In the Middle of the Mess*:

> Having a moment of pure joy in a restroom in Ayr, Scotland, was a gift, but I had to learn how to make that a daily practice. So, as I felt the darkness closing in, I chose a place to meet with God every day, to bring my darkness into the light. It wasn't something I added to my to-do list; it was simply my daily who-I-am place.
>
> I began to sit on the little patio in our back garden, by the fountain where the water gushes from a lion's mouth. I began to meet my Father every day in a fresh, intimate way. I was at the beginning of a new adventure with God. I brought my Bible, a journal, a pen, a hymnbook, a large cup of coffee, and a worship playlist on my iPhone. And morning after morning, I brought the secret lies I believed into God's light. I listened as He reminded me that even in the darkness of my depression, I was well-loved.
>
> I still go to that chair in the morning. Some mornings I'll read from the hymnbook and let the words wash over me.
>
> O Love that wilt not let me go,
> I rest my weary soul in thee;
> I give thee back the life I owe,
> That in thine ocean depths its flow
> May richer, fuller be.

O light that followest all my way,
I yield my flickering torch to thee;
My heart restores its borrowed ray,
That in thy sunshine's blaze its day
May brighter, fairer be.

O Joy that seekest me through pain,
I cannot close my heart to thee;
I trace the rainbow through the rain,
And feel the promise is not vain,
That morn shall tearless be.

What might you gain from establishing such a place in your daily rhythm, and in your heart?

What is keeping you from going there now?

And now these three remain: faith, hope and love.
But the greatest of these is love.

—PAUL (1 CORINTHIANS 13:13)

PRACTICING THE DISCIPLINE OF LIVING LIGHT

We have reached the spiritual discipline to which all other disciplines point: choosing light at every turn. We can be freed from this brokenness that has bound us up. We can know victory over suffering and death. We can seek righteousness, prize unity, and rest in God's grace. We can step forward from darkness to light. We can be *fearless* regarding the troubles that long to take us down. And we can begin living this way *today*.

1. Reconfirm Your Commitment to God

To practice "living light," find a recording of the hymn, "O Love that Wilt Not Let Me Go" by George Matheson, that Sheila quotes at the end of the *In the Middle of the Mess* book excerpt on pages 178–179. Listen to the song as you reread the lyrics. In your mind, in your heart, and in your soul, reconfirm your commitment before God to "yield" your "flickering torch" to Him. Spend several minutes in quiet conversation with your Father, trading your heavy burden for His burden so light, assuming your posture of belovedness before Him, and being settled by His great grace.

2. Confess Any Lack of Peace

Confess to God the aspects of your earthly experience that lack peace today. Ask Him to give you glimpses of our coming reality, which you can begin to practice now.

3. Commit to Love Well

Lay before God your earnest desire to love well, in your relationship to Him, in your relationship to yourself, and in your relationship to those whom He has placed in your life. Those who are loved well love well . . . so ask Him to remind you of His deep-and-wide love for you.

4. Move Forward from Brokenness

Emerge from your time of contemplation with fresh resolve to accept what is broken, grieve the losses you've absorbed, speak truth to God and others, and say *thank you* for gains already made. On page 182, journal some of your thoughts as you close this study.

And remember, the sense of "all-rightness" you've been searching for has found you at last. As Sheila said in this session's video segment, "You are loved—wildly so. You are loved, and you are not alone." God is with you, and that is permanent. May every broken place find its wholeness in Him.

Leader's Guide

Thank you for agreeing to lead a small group through this study! What you have chosen to do is valuable and will make a great difference in the lives of others.

In the Middle of the Mess is a six-session study built around video content and small-group interaction. As the group leader, just think of yourself as the host of a dinner party. Your job is to take care of your guests by managing all the behind-the-scenes details so that when everyone arrives, they can just enjoy time together.

As the group leader, your role is not to answer all the questions or re-teach the content—the video, book, and study guide will do most of that work. Your job is to guide the experience and create an environment where people can process, question, and reflect—not receive more instruction.

Make sure everyone in the group gets a copy of the study guide. This will keep everyone on the same page and help the process run more smoothly. If some group members are unable to purchase the guide, arrange it so that people can share the resource with other group members. Giving everyone access to all the material will position this study to be as rewarding an experience as possible. Everyone should feel free to write in their study guides and bring them to group every week.

Setting Up the Group

As the group leader, you'll want to create an environment that encourages sharing and learning. A church sanctuary or formal classroom may not be as ideal as a living room, because those locations can feel formal and less intimate. No matter what setting you choose, provide enough comfortable seating for everyone, and, if possible, arrange the seats in a semicircle so everyone can see the video easily. This will make the transition between the video and group conversation more efficient and natural.

Try to get to the meeting site early so you can greet the group members as they arrive. Simple refreshments create a welcoming atmosphere and can be a wonderful addition to a group study evening. Be sure to take food and pet allergies into account to make your guests as comfortable as possible. You may also want to consider offering childcare to couples with children who want to attend. Finally, be sure your media technology is working properly. Managing these details up front will make the rest of your group experience flow smoothly and provide a welcoming space in which to engage the content of *In the Middle of the Mess*.

Starting Your Group Time

Once everyone has arrived, it's time to begin the group. Here are some simple tips to make your group time healthy, enjoyable, and effective.

First, consider beginning the meeting with a short prayer, and remind the group members to silence their phones. This is a way to make sure you can all be present with one another and with God.

Next, give each person one to two minutes to respond to the question(s) in the "Opening Thoughts" section. Usually, you won't answer the discussion questions yourself, but you should go first with the "Opening Thoughts" question(s), answering briefly and with a reasonable amount of transparency.

Let the group members know that sharing is optional, and it's no problem if they can't get to some of the between-sessions questions and activities some weeks. It will still be beneficial for them to hear from the other group members and learn about what they discovered.

Leading the Discussion Time

Now that the group is engaged, it's time to watch the video and respond with some directed small-group discussion. Encourage all the group members to participate in the discussion, but make sure they know they don't have to do so. As the discussion progresses, you may want to follow up with comments such as, "Tell me more about that," or, "Why did you answer that way?" This will allow the group members to deepen their reflections and invite meaningful sharing in a nonthreatening way.

Note that you have been given multiple questions to use in each session, and you do not have to use them all or even follow them in order. Feel free to pick and choose questions based on either the needs of your group or how the conversation is flowing. Also, don't be afraid of silence. Offering a question and allowing up to thirty seconds of silence is okay. It allows people space to think about how they want to respond and also gives them time to do so.

As group leader, you are the boundary keeper for your group. Do not let anyone (yourself included) dominate the group time. Keep an eye out for group members who might be tempted to "attack" folks they disagree with or try to "fix" those having struggles. These kinds of behaviors can derail a group's momentum, so they need to be steered in a different direction. Model active listening and encourage everyone in your group to do the same. This will make your group time a safe space and create a positive community.

Allow enough time at the end of your gathering for prayer, using the prayer prompt provided if you desire. Also, encourage everyone to dig deeper into the session's theme by doing the between-sessions personal study, which is rich in reflection, Bible exploration, and the practice of a spiritual discipline. There will be opportunity to share insights or questions about that time at the start of the next session.

Thank you again for taking the time to lead your group. You are making a difference in the lives of others and having an impact on the kingdom of God.

About the Author

Sheila Walsh is a Scottish lass known as "the encourager" to the more than 5.5 million women she's met and spoken to around the world. She loves being a Bible teacher, making God's Word practical, and sharing her own story of how God met her when she was at her lowest point and lifted her up again.

Sheila also enjoys being an author—in fact, she likes to write every day—and has sold more than 5 million books. She is the cohost of the television program *Life Today* with James and Betty Robison, airing in the United States, Canada, Europe, and Australia.

Calling Texas home, Sheila lives in Dallas with her husband, Barry; her son, Christian; and three little dogs—Belle, Tink, and Maggie.

You can stay in touch at

sheilawalsh.com

facebook.com/sheilawalshconnects

Instagram @sheilawalsh1